PREFACE

The need of having a sports series felt because today's situation of the world is not conducive to peace, all round there is destruction, despair, conflict and war; war if not between two nations then within the country itself. In a world where there are some 820 million people unemployed or under-employed, and where 86 million people are born every year, it is not surprising that one out of every four individuals lives in absolute poverty. The *Discovery Publishing House* by Publishing this series seeks to get positive response as—to means by which sports can promote and propagate peace and international cooperation. Sportsmen form a large identifiable cadre. We visualises a situation where a conscious efforts is made all over the world to train the sportspersons to spread the message of peace and international cooperation. Instead of peace keeping efforts through arms and army, the sportspersons may be used as soldiers of peace in a subtle manner. The effort is to make the realize the contribution of sports as a factor for sustainable development, peace keeping and international cooperation.

In developing countries, sports development cooperation is still in the need of justification and steadfast arguments. Many people ask the question "why invest in sports in developing countries for which water supply, health service and agriculture projects are much better suited? An apt reply to this question may be "for many of the people of a developing country,

Sports is the only 'Sweaty' Leisure-time activity. Sports represents a moment of joy in the midst of hard poverty-stricken and dirty everyday life. Doing sports even makes one's work go more smoothly the next day.

This series will be useful to the sports promoters, organisers, coaches and other persons related or interested in sports.

Editor

CONTENTS

1

INTRODUCTION

Hockey is one of the many sports derived from pre-historic man's delight in stick and ball games which gave the world such varied pursuits as the English Cricket, American Baseball and Persian Polo. Its birth place was Asia and authorities credit Persia with having devised it about 2000 B.C. It is said that The Greeks and the Romans played hockey but nothing is known about the nature of the game that they played. The earliest mention of the present day game dates back only to 1527, when the Galway Statutes included hockey, the horlinge of litill balle with... sticks or staves in a list of prohibited games.

Modern hockey, as created in England, resembles most closely games once popular in the British Isles and no doubt, hockey's immediate forerunners were the Scottish shinty, the English and Welsh bandy and the Irish hurling. But it is generally assumed that the true ancestor of hockey was hurling. Hurling crossed the sea from Irin to England to be assimilated into the English way of life, eventually to become hockey.

The first hockey club was formed in Blackheath in 1861. The sticks were made of oak and the end position was teamed and then pressed to give it a hooked shape. The ball was a solid cube of rubber with rounded corners.

Hockey became one of the games so enthusiastically taken up that the government became perturbed that it would interfere with men's national service as archers. Hockey was therefore included in a ban, issued by King Edward III in 1365, which is the first definite record of the existence of the game in Britain. It was then still called bandy ball. Landowners who nevertheless permitted playing of the game on their property, faced a fine of $20 and three years' imprisonment. With the passage of time, the game became more refined and civilized, Among the earliest refinements introduced was the prohibition of raising the head of the stick above shoulder level. Any player who struck his opponent either with the stick or his hand faced immediate suspension. The game was standardised by the Wimbledon Hockey Club in 1883. Its regulations (adopted in 1886 by the Hockey Association) thoroughly modernised the sport, making it highly scientific and skillful.

The first international match was held in 1895 between England and Ireland. In 1980 hockey was included in the modern Olympic Games. Perhaps the most extraordinary aspect of its evolution is that a game once so rough and unruly, was adopted by women.

Hockey became popular in India when the British Regiments played the game in India and introduced it in the British Indian Regiments who quickly picked up the game. The first hockey club was formed in Calcutta in 1885-86 followed by Bombay and Punjab. The Bengal Hockey was the first Hockey Association in India founded in 1908. The second was formed in 1920 in Karachi by the name 'Sind Hockey Association'.

With the popularity of the game, associations were formed in different states—Bombay, Bihar, Orissa and Delhi.

In Olympic Games India played hockey for the first time in 1928 held in Amsterdam. She reached the final defeating Austria, Belgium, Denmark and Switzerland. In the final match, India defeated Holland by three goals to nil. In was an exciting match, India's first Olympic entry in Hockey culminating in victory gave the Indian Hockey Federation a name and reputation which it has since maintained. Women in India have also been taken up to Hockey. Their standard of play is fairly good but they lack stamina and do not play a fast game. A women's hockey team from Ceylon visited India in January 1967 and played five test matches. India won all the 'test series'. In January 1968, the first Asian Women's Hockey Championship was held in New Delhi. India lost to Japan and Uganda.

A game shall be played between two teams of not more than 16 players each. Not more than eleven players of each team shall be on the field of play at the same time. Each team shall have one goalkeeper on the field or shall indicate a field player who has the privileges of a goalkeeper (also known as a kicking back). Each team is permitted to substitute from a maximum of 16 players. There is no limit to the number of players from the same team who may be substituted at the same time. A player who has been substituted may re-enter the field of play as a substitute for another player. No substitute shall be permitted for a suspended player during his suspension. When a suspended player's suspension is complete, he may be substituted without first returning to the pitch. (i) The substitution of players may take place at any time other than following the award of a penalty corner or penalty corner or penalty stroke subject to (ii) below.

After the award of a penalty corner or penalty stroke any player who is incapacitated and has to leave the field of play can be substituted subject to Rules. In the event of the defending goalkeeper being incapacitated he shall be replaced immediately by another goalkeeper. If the defending goalkeeper be suspended, his team captain shall immediately nominate another goalkeeper. Replacement goal-keepers shall be permitted to put on, without wasting time, protective equipment. Time shall not be stopped while substitutions are made other than for incapacitated players.

Players entering the field before the players being substituted have left the field should be penalised in accordance. The duration of the game shall be two periods of thirty-five minutes each, unless otherwise agreed before the game. At half-time the teams shall change ends, and the duration of the interval shall not exceed five minutes, unless otherwise agreed before the game, but in no case shall it exceed ten minutes. The game starts when the umpire blows his whistle for the opening passback.

Let us assume that you have mastered the technical and tactical skills of hockey and have the speed and stamina and every other qualification required of a good player. To give of your best you should be able to play independently keeping your proper position and making quick and correct decisions on the field. In order to do these things well you have to develop will-power and much temperament, without which a player, however good he may be, will be a failure in big games.

Players usually have their own physical training schedules. But what you do on the day of the match is of utmost importance. There is the case of a team which, after beating a strong side in the first round of a tournament in a port town unaccountably lost of much weaker opposition in the second round. It had transpired earlier in the day that a majority of the team, coming as they did from an inland town, could not resist the temptation of a swim in the sea. They were a tired side even before they took field.

It is important that a player does not do anything out of the ordinary daily schedule on the day of a match. Avoid going to bed late in the previous night. The usual reason for late-nights are pictures, dances and drinking. Avoid all three. A player, in order to give to his best, should finish his mid-day meal at least five hours before the match. Light refreshment, say a cup of tea and a couple of biscuits or sandwiches, an hour before the match would be ideal. Avoid overeating or heavy food.

Reach the ground well in time. Experience shows the players hurrying to the ground just in the nick of time are in no state to give of their best. Do a few warming up and limbering exercises before entering the field. The whole team should be in the field a few minutes before the whistle for the bully. In these minutes let the forwards have some shots at the goalkeeper in order to get confidence, the other players also practising what they are supposed to do in the game. In the interval players should refresh themselves in a way which suits them best. Some like a hot beverage, others prefer to suck a lemon or ice. Drinking water at half time is not a good habit. The coach, captain and the other players should also utilise the time to discuss the game, giving encouragement and advice where it is needed.

Mr. S.M. Macildowie, a prominent member of International Hockey Rules Board of Federation International de Hockey, has expressed his views on the subject given below. It is interesting and informative for the readers:

The reason for playing Hockey

It may surprise some employers of hockey to know that the real objects of playing hockey are:

(a) To provide relaxation from the ardours of the previous week's work, and build one up for the following week's grind,

(b) To provide a pleasant form of exercise to keep one in a good state of physical fitness, and

(c) To give one an opportunity of enjoyment the benefits of sun and fresh air, and

(d) To make hockey friends, and widen ones knowledge of our worthy colleagues.

In fact, work is alas, a necessity, to keep the wheels of life going, whereas hockey is optional, enjoyable, exhilarating and sociable. If we lose out at work then indeed we have to worry; as other work has to be found, but if we lose at hockey, nothing material is lost, the next game will still happen and the same degree of pleasure will be available. Unfortunately in many cases these days players of hockey seem to have forgotten this fact, and are treating work and hockey on a par degree of seriousness in life. By this I do not suggest that one should not play to win, quite the reverse, one should, if necessary, be so tried that a stretcher is needed to remove the body to the changing room. If a player can honestly say he cannot run another yard and has throughout played good and clean hockey, then the result is quite unimportant.

2

PRACTICE METHODS

Advanced skills

Observation of a top-level game will reveal diversity of style and a wide range of stickwork, usually built up through years of practice and experimentation. Individuals can be seen to vary from a rigidly functional approach to the other extreme of sheer artistry. The final style which an individual evolves is influenced by the basic teaching received; her physical attributes and deficiencies; whether or not she has tried to emulate another player; and her desire to continue perfecting her skill for its own sake. Real mastery only develops when a player is not only motivated by the need to be effective, but also by an aesthetic appreciation of the skills under her control.

Skills should be so well learned that they can survive pressure and retain their effectiveness. There is a tendency for players who are pressured to resort to those skills in which they have greatest confidence. They become less willing to take risks and this limited approach to the game makes their play more predictable and more easily counteracted. Observation will also reinforce the point that the real experts are more consistent and their skill can withstand the pressure of increased competition, unlike lesser performers who find this more difficult. It is a great asset for a player to be confident in her own ability even when those around her are lapsing into mediocrity.

In hockey we are concerned not only with skilled actions but also the way in which these skills are applied. Skill involves, therefore, not only technical expertise, but also are ability to adapt one's responses and assess beforehand the needs of the situation. The player may need to release the ball immediately on receiving it or maintain possession while creating or waiting for a more suitable moment. Thus decision-making becomes important because the player needs to pay attention to the picture of the whole game, make rapid judgements, select the appropriate response and then act. It is obviously an advantage to be able to select a response from a wide repertoire in order to meed the demands or the situation as accurately as possible.

Skill is functional in that it is designed and produced to achieve a known objective, and the success of that skilled action is determined by how nearly the original intention is achieved. For example, success in placing a pass is judged by how closely it approaches the target. Thus if we accept that skilled actions in hockey are purposeful and goal-directed, and not merely expressive, we can also categorize these skills and assess them objectively in terms of success or failure.

If skills are to be goal-directed, they must be related to tactics. Remember tactics are present as soon as an individual player matches her skill against an opponent and the successful exploitation of any tactical situation depends on good reading of the game and the ability to perform the skills which are necessary to achieve the tactical objective. It is important to understand the interpretation given to the word "skill". Skill involves the peculiar abilities of each player, linked with good timing and the appropriate application of techniques to the game. Techniques, on the other hand, are specific skilled actions. The drive is a good example where the combination of footwork and the manipulation of the stick and ball produces a pattern which is easily recognizable.

Techniques can be executed in isolation or they can be part of a sequence of actions where the effectiveness of each succeeding action depends upon what had gone before. Accumulated errors in such a sequence call for greater adaptation and consequently higher levels of skill. The good player who can, by her skill in receiving, make a bad pass look good is a prize example.

Each player is endowed with certain abilities which effect the level of proficiency attainable. Players develop attitudes towards skills which influence their approach to the game. Young players who are currently finding their way into selected teams, by their approach to the game, advertise the way they have been taught and the types of pitch on which they acquired their technical expertise. Those who have developed on a fast, artificial surface frequently display delicacy of stick control, but all too often they approach the ball with the intention to push, when a drive would be more suitable. A habit forms, and their game lacks the power which is so essential at times.

Another factor which can affect the proficiency of

a player is the choice of stick. Acquisition of hockey techniques can be made easier by using a stick which is of suitable size and weight. Contrary to popular belief a heavier stick does not necessarily increase the power of the drive since the speed of the swing is more influential. A player with a lighter stick does not need to work so hard on the swing itself nor does she need to carry the extra weight, sometimes in one hand, for the seventy minutes of the game; hence, a lower expenditure of energy. A longer stick should not be chosen with the claim that it extends the reach of the player. Good footwork should solve that problem. A thick handle in relation to the hand size is not advisable as it tends to produce rigidity in the wrists, and this prevents the stick from twisting in the hands, which in turn makes manipulation of the head of the stick more difficult. Ideally the fingers should be able to close around the handle. Dexterity is essential. If the head of the stick is too thick it can restrict the ability to lift the ball in the scoop, flick or fling strokes.

The game of hockey makes two demands with regard to skill: namely, consistency and adaptability. Hitting a stationary ball at a corner to an exact spot requires the former. This can be practised quite easily as the objective is clear. Success is easily measurable and it is appropriate that the action becomes almost automatic so that it can be repeated exactly on future occasions. After regular practice by many players a corner -hitting expert may emerge to take over the role habitually given to wing players. In this way an individual's specific skill may be used to the mutual advantage of the whole team.

Superb thing is one of the hallmarks of the highly

skilled performer for even if a player anticipates another's intentions, accurate timing is still needed for the skill to be effective. A player's thoughts and actions must be in harmony in the same way that her skill must match the speed of her ability to make decisions in circumstances where speed is vital. The ability to read the game quickly may enable a player to have more time to respond in some circumstances, thereby giving the impressions of being unhurried. One factor very evident in good players is alertness: that acute interest in all that happens around them. Reading the game is make easier when a player is highly skilled for she is able to withdraw her conscious awareness from the actual execution of the stroke and focus it on changes occurring during the game.

Returning to the observation of a top-class game, it is evident that skilled performance displays economy of effort, quicker responses, greater accuracy, fluency and the impression of having plenty of time to deal with the situation. Combining alertness, knowledge of the game and skill, a player is rarely caught unawares. This may be one reason why spectators following some top-level games are heard to express disappointment at the lack of flair or to proclaim the game dull. In highly skilled games it is likely that there will be fewer surprises because everybody is reading the game well in advance, is prepared for what is to come and is equipped to deal with it. There is a levelling out of ability which means that one player can rarely show superiority over another. In a closely matched game, attacking breakthrough tend to be a direct result of errors on the part of the defenders. A good player in a lower-level game can beat a number of players at will, but when matched against those of equal ability and experience she has to do much more to be successful. It is vital that she is prepared mentally and physically to meet such a challenge. Thus, when learning techniques is essential to acquire them in a way that is closely related to the game and at the maximum controlled speed.

Fitness is an essential part of the game. Techniques deteriorate as fatigue increases so players must work to improve their strength, speed and stamina. Many games are won or lost in the final minutes and it would be tragic to lose a game because players were too unfit to perform the skills they have practised so long. Fitness is specific to each individual but most players need to add activities to their training which will help their bodies to meet the demands to be made on them. Carefully planned practice sessions with stick and ball can go a long way towards producing the required level of fitness and it is advisable, using pressure practices, to combine stickwork with fitness training.

Practice methods

'Practice' can be defined as any activity which a player undertakes in order to try to modify or consolidate skilled actions. Simple repetition of an action is not enough, for all practice should stress quality. Quantity alone is not sufficient, and indeed the practice of wrong movements may only serve to confirm bad habits and so be detrimental. Normally it is accepted that shorter, more frequent practice sessions are most beneficial, but if the criterion of quality is applied, then it can be seen that length and distribution of practice sessions will be determined by how much a player can absorb and how long she can sustain the standard of the practice. Different procedures may be adopted according to the objectives of the coaching session and the ability of the players taking part. Basically three situations emerge.

The first of these arises when the players are able to produce a recognizable version of the whole technique immediately after attending to instructions and seeing a visual demonstration, and are able to modify subsequent repetitions to eliminate any faults present in the initial attempt. This is really only possible where the skills involved are fairly simple or well within the scope of the players concerned. When observing the efforts made it is important for the coach to be able to differentiate between the desirable elements of a skilled performance and those elements which will detract from efficiency. This method of working on the whole action should be adopted where possible because it allows maximum activity and, providing it falls within the ability range of the players once they have seen the picture of the whole action as it is sufficient to allow them to copy the demonstration and then evaluate the results. Then the coach and the player can identify faults which recur over the first few attempts. Remember the initial effort is rarely typical and do not fall into the trap of making your diagnosis too early. Individual remedies then need to be provided. When a large group is involved the most common faults will need to be identified and coped with first while the few individuals who a re encountering particular problems are dealt with separately. Where more than one fault exists these should be ranked in priority order and the most basic one dealt with first since the correction of one fault may contribute to the elimination of others.

The second situation is one in which the players have achieved a reasonable level of competence, but where faults persist. As the fault cannot be eliminated through repeating the whole action it is necessary to isolate the fault and employ a corrective practice. When this is successful the modified part is absorbed into whole action. For example, in the fling stroke a player may be getting lift and length, but insufficient spin because of poor wrist action. The player can slow the whole action down by placing the head of the stick underneath the ball and by lifting the ball higher initially while effecting the correct wrist action.

Success or failure can be assessed by noting the reaction of the ball in flight and also its reaction against the ground. The practice is made easier by removing the power required to gain length, and reintroducing it later. If success is not realised it may be necessary for further corrective measures to be applied. A discerning coach may speed up the learning process by more skilful analysis which enables her to select the most appropriate procedure from a pool of corrective measures. The coach needs to have a number of different remedies at her fingertips to suit the needs of individual players. Really individual coaching is essential here because of shortage of time and the need for close guidance throughout the practice period. Frequently players who are already fairly competent are reluctant to work on minor discrepancies and they need to see the long term benefits to be gained if they are to be motivated to make a real effort.

The third situation is one in which players are trying to acquire complex technique which are too difficult for them to experience early success. It may be necessary to build up the technique in progressive stages where the skill is learnt as a series of interrelated actions which eventually combine to produce the whole action. Few isolated techniques in hockey are so complex as to demand this type of practice, but it is beneficial where isolated actions are linked together to produce a sequence of events, where additional problems are involved in mastering the transitions between the separate actions and where timing becomes particularly influential. For example, a player may need to run to receive the ball and swerve as contact is made, followed by an immediate checking of the movement to reposition and shoot for goal. Receiving, swerving, checking and shooting can all be practised separately and then they are chained together in the correct order and the sequence progressively acquired.

Structuring practices

Practices should be planned bearing the following points in mid:

(a) The simplest, clearest possible structure should be designed to achieve the required objective.

(b) Adequate space should be provided. Players cannot concentrate on the matter in hand if they are conscious of having to avoid other people.

(c) A realistic playing surface is advisable. The first attempt at any technique greatly influences future development. Therefore, it is unwise to learn to scoop off a hard surface or try to develop close dribbling at speed in thick mud and long grass.

(d) Ample equipment should be available so that time

is not lost collecting balls, for example, when practising corner hitting.

(e) Practices should be orientated towards the normal direction of play when a pitch is being used.

(f) Optimum size of groups should be used to ensure maximum practice of the specific technique. For example, a player learning to fling a ball needs only a pile of balls and a fence. A player practising the double technique of 'receive and pass' can play the major role in a group of three. Player A feeds a ball to player B, who has to find moving target player C, who collects the ball. This is repeated and all three players are getting practice in passing and receiving, but only one player is combining the two actions. This is a rotation practice which means that the players move round to work in each of three positions following a given number of repetitions. It is advisable when structuring the size of groups to avoid moving from twos to threes because of the time taken to regroup. This can be speeded up, if it is necessary, by forming twos into sixes and then dividing the large group in half.

(g) Practices should be continuous or repeated after each attempt.

(h) The current ability of the players should be considered for this will largely determine the space they need, the amount of pressure which can be applied and the number of consecutive turns which can be expected before fatigue sets in. In more advanced coaching one can expect players to do much of this organisation for themselves. The lower the level of ability the more detailed the organisation needs to be.

Pressure practices

These are used to simulate a harder situation than the one anticipated during the game, so that the actual event feels comparatively easy. Pressure can be applied through the restriction is equivalent to the presence of opposition. Pressure practices can be designed for individuals and for groups. For example, when working as an individual, a player can use a wall as a partner. She can run parallel to it, driving the ball on to it an angle, meeting it from the rebound, carrying it and driving again. A simple example of imposing pressure of time can be seen when two players each with a ball start simultaneously side by side and dribble in a race to a line 10 yd. away on which the ball must be stopped.

Pressure practices frequently involve putting a player in the hot seat and the following example illustrates this. Three players are involved. Players A and B each have a ball. Player C is positioned about 10 yd (9.14 m.) in front of them. A drives the ball straight ahead of herself, C moves sideways to collect it and returns it to A. Player B drives her ball straight ahead of herself whilst C is recovering to her central position. C meets this ball and returns it to B before immediately recovering to meet the second drive from player A. This is repeated for as long as player C can keep the practice going. The receiver should aim to run with her shoulders facing the feeders all the time. Time pressure can be increased by strengthening the drive, by increasing the sideways distance the receiver has to cover, by shortening the distance between the receiver and the feeders or by the feeders releasing the ball earlier. The drive, fling or push strokes can be used in this practice. The final example is devised around a restriction of space. Confined to an area 4 yd. (3.66 m.) square two players are given possession of the ball and an opponent introduced who attempts to get the ball. The two players must keep the ball within the square and are allowed to pass or dodge in order to avoid the opponent. They are not allowed to break any rules applicable in the full game of hockey.

Pressure practices are designed to be physically demanding as well as exacting in terms of the skill required to make them work effectively. They should be interspersed with less vigorous activities if players are to derive maximum benefit from them.

A coach frequently faces a dilemma when coaching experienced players. Namely, whether or not to try to strengthen a player's technical weakness or consolidate on her strengths. It is evident that in working on the weakness, the strengths can deteriorate and so it may be more beneficial to structure the team tactics to make the most of her strengths and hide her weaknesses. It is well known that old habits die hard and a great deal of time is required if skills are to be broken down and restructured to advantage.

The following guidelines might be worthy of attention in the coaching of technique.

(a) Cover a wide range of skills as early as possible. The ease or difficulty of different techniques must be released to each player and it is likely that there will be personal differences. Do not tell a player that a skill is difficult before she attempts it, and remember that mastery of difficult skills may make simpler skills easier to learn.

(b) In addition to the visual information which is

available to the performer the coach must provide criticism to enable a player to make accurate adjustments both prior to and during the repetition of an action. For example a player may see her drive fail to reach its target. She can see the results of her efforts, but she may not know why the ball went astray. This is where the coach can provide a verbal comment such as 'keep the left shoulder pointing towards the target until the stroke is completed.' This can be reinforced during the next attempt by the coach instructing the player as she repeats the action and in helping her with the timing. Later attempts may only require the work 'shoulder' as a reminder before leaving the player to consolidate the corrected action.

(c) Incentives for success such as selection for a national team may already exist and motivation must be moderated accordingly. A player already concerned about her ability to make the grade may become over anxious if motivated too strongly, resulting in deterioration of performance.

(d) Initially, techniques may be learnt in isolation, especially in they are complex and if the player already shows some lack of confidence in the game, but as soon as possible practice should become realistic and applied directly to the game. It is essential for a player to learn not only the technique but how her execution of it fits into the whole pattern of the game.

(e) Once the pattern of the action is established it should be speeded up to the maximum controlled speed which can be coped with by each individual.

(f) Because hockey skills are perceptual, in that they are displayed in response to stimuli from the game, the players need to learn how to search the game for information and this necessitates their attention being drawn from the actual execution of the technique on occasions. This is only possible if the skills are so well learnt that they can be done without the need for conscious control.

(g) Only the most important information should be given to a learner before she has a go. She needs to have a mental picture of the finished product and to understand what it is designed to achieve, and she needs to receive only one or two points on which she can concentrate while practising.

(h) When an error is made, the player should not be allowed to repeat this or it may become established. Some modification must occur, based on information offered by the coach or collected by the player herself on the evidence of the results of the action.

(i) Where a player finds difficulty in complying with an instruction from a coach it is sometimes beneficial to draw the attention of the learner away from her own feeling of whether or not she is doing the right thing and towards structuring the environment so that only the right action can be completed. For example, use the proximity of a wall to restrict the size of the backlift in the drive.

(j) Speed and accuracy are interrelated. It is important to decide whether speed or accuracy should receive most stress when learning a skill. Where speed is essential to the success of the action then it is unwise to practise that skill slowly, but where accuracy is crucial, practice at a slower pace can be more beneficial for a time, knowing that it is not always to take time to be careful during the game.

One of the difficulties of coaching techniques is that they are governed by an adherence to certain principles in order to be effective. Good style, instead of being the product of the personal expression of those principles, is thought by some to be merely the decoration on the cake. Good style involves doing the basic actions well with economy of effort and it is largely enhanced by perfect timing. Individual preferences for range and speed of movement establish the style of each player. Every player is free to express her skills in her own way, but the unnecessary flourish with the stick or some idiosyncrasy of footwork or posture can, at top level, be a disadvantage if these advertise the intentions of the player, especially where deception is required. On the other hand, much interest would be lost from the game if such variations in style were smothered. Individually and flair are to be encouraged providing they are constructed on the basic framework which will offer the best chance of success.

Techniques, then, are developed to enable players to use tactics and so, as well as being proficient in a wide range of skills, each individual will also develop a personal repertoire of skills which are peculiar to her playing position and the role she is expected to play in team, and which suit her strengths and weakness.

Here are four examples. A left halfback has to be able to tackle from the non-stick side in order to keep between her opponent and the goal. She may opt for any of the following methods: one, a jab tackle; two, a circular tackle; three, a one-handed reverse stick tackle; four, a two-handed reverse stick tackle. She is able to choose her angle of approach and the choice of tackle may be largely determined by her speed in relation to that of her opponent, or the strength of her left wrist. Thus, although a choice of methods is available, the final choice is determined by the needs of the situation, the abilities and preferences of the players concerned, and by the movement which is to follow the successful completion of the tackle. A centre-forward needs to develop especially close ball control in a confined space in addition to immediate and effective changes of pace and the ability to dribble fairly long distances at high speed. Defenders frequently need to control and clear the ball with as little hesitation as possible.

The position into which a player settles should reflect the majority of her strengths, although she is likely to have some weakness which need to be hidden or improved. An established right wing who finds difficulty in hitting hard to the right as she rarely has to use it, may avoid interchanging to a large extent. Such specialization in positional play is limiting and may hinder a player's advancement as she cannot be used elsewhere.

Analysis of techniques

The techniques will be considered in detail according to their function and methods of practice. The following principles underlie all the strokes and a concentration on these will help in the development of an effective technique:

(a) The importance of footwork before, during and after the stroke;

(b) Utilization of power from the legs and hips when maximum force is required;

(c) Keeping the head over the ball at the moment of contract.

(d) A compact preparation which retains control of the head of the stick;

(e) A follow-through a aid fluency, help maintain power and direction;

(f) Use of a suitable grip which varies with the stroke and to some extent with individual preference.

Travelling with the ball

Dribbling is used to enable a player to cover ground with the ball in her possession, as a preparation for other strokes-for example, when manoeuvring to pass or shoot, to move away from an attempted tackle, or to accelerate into a space and so draw a defended away from a crowded area.

The techniques required vary according to the needs of the situation. Normally we encourage players to concentrate on maintaining close control where the ball is kept on the stick and steered in the desired direction. This push dribble necessitates continuous contact with the ball which is essential when moving in confined spaces. However, if a player is less pressured and wishes to cover ground more quickly, then contact with the ball is likely to be more spasmodic, especially when the playing surface is poor. Indeed, when there is a clear space ahead the ball may be deliberately hit forward, chased and collected, as a player without the ball can travel faster than a player with the ball.

Four techniques for dribbling should be considered. Players on the left of the field anticipating the need to pass right should acquire a 'drag' dribble whereby the feet run slightly ahead of the ball. This shorten the preparation required to pass right, enabling a player to disguise the intended pass more easily as it will be completed in a shorter time. The preparatory movements are reduced to a pivot of the feet and a twist in the body to bring the left shoulder round to point towards the target. Players on the right of the field anticipating the need to pass to the left should dribble the ball in front of the feet so that it can be guided quickly to the left foot before the pass is made. The ability to main close control while swerving in different directions is a prerequisite for evading opponents and is facilitated by dribbling with the ball in front of the feet allowing for an immediate movement to either side. This can be accomplished more easily by employing an alternate orthodox and reverse stick dribble where the ball travels on a zigzag. This is used mostly to confuse approaching defenders.

If a player is crouched too low over the stick, she will not be able to run freely and will limit the amount she can see. If players are taught to dribble with the hands apart on the stick there is a tendency for them to drop the right hand too low, so it may be better to start them dribbling with the hands apart on the stick there is a tendency for them to drop the right hand too low, so it may be better to start them dribbling with the hands together at the top of the stick and then encourage them to lower the right hand a few inches, until they feel they have better control. Do this while they are running as quickly as they can manage, then introduce swerving round obstacles, stopping and starting quickly, swerving round moving players in a confined space, and accelerating and decelerating without losing control.

Passing

Accuracy in passing

A player stands in the middle of a 15 yards square and the other three players stand at the corners of square No. 1, 3 and 4. Player No. 1 in a corner starts the game by passing the ball to the inside player who, in return, is required to beat one of the two remaining players. Both players are required to change their position from No. 3 corner to No. 4 and No. 4 corner player to No. 1 just after the start of the game. The inside player tries to pass the ball at one of the two corners No. 1 and 4.

A player is beaten who fails to stop the ball before crossing the ball at his corner and changes his position with the inside player. The starter of the game positioning at No. 1 corner has to move at corner No. 2 after passing the ball to the inside player. Before starting the next game he sure that No. 2 corner is kept always free without a player. All players should also play inside the square turn by turn to complete the exercise. This exercise ensures the accuracy in passing and improving the speed of the players.

There are four players at the corner and the fifth player is inside the square of 15 yards. Player at No. 1 corner is with the ball who starts the game with a pass to the inside player. With the start of the game all the four players move to their next corner in an anticlockwise direction. The inside player, after receiving the ball, tries to beat one of the four players who is still on his way. The player is beaten if the ball crosses the corner before he stops it and changes his position with the inside players.

Before the completion of the exercise every player has played inside the square. In a fifteen yards square three players stand on the line and pass to each other without entering the square. A player inside the square intercepts the passes. The player whose pass is intercepted changes his position with the inside player. Players on the line should pass in an unoccupied place in order to develop such a habit of understanding among themselves.

The correct way of receiving a pass

One player passes and the other receives it. The receiver, after controlling the ball, moves a few steps ahead and then returns the ball to the first player who repeats it. Both the players pass to each other well away and on either side of them. With a view to avoiding the infringement of Obstruction the receiver trap the ball while facing towards his opponents' goal. In case the ball come to the left side within a controllable speed, he should grab the ball with a reverse stick and if it is on the right side the ball should be stopped with a reverse stick when it comes just ahead of him.

Receiving a pass at an unexpected place

Two players face each other with a distance of 15 to 20 yards between them and try to catch each other on the wrong foot by passing in unexpected directions 8 to 10 yards away from the receiver. This practice develops the habit to return the ball immediately by the player.

Reverse flick pass

Players with the ball on the left side dribble the ball

from a distance of 10 yards and pass with the reverse flick to the opposite player lined up on the right side. The right side player, after shooting at the goal, return to join the line of the left side players to practise the reverse flick.

Here the shooters are required to allow the ball to come to their right side to have a good angle for shooting at the goal.

Back pass

The left winger finds himself unable to beat the opponent defender or to make his game easier gets assistance from his wing-half by giving a back pass to him who returns the ball in the gap by giving a through pass to the left winger.

The attacking player does not find a gap between three defenders lined up in front of him. He passes the ball back to his half-back who returns the ball to him from the gap.

Players line up on the right side pass the ball inside the circle and ahead of the left side player to take a shot at the goal. Such passes are profitable than the direct passes.

Passes in open spaces

The No. 1 player is with the ball who passes it on No. 2 at an uncovered place. The No. 2 player who has an understanding with player No. 1, moves towards that direction before the pass reaches him. After receiving the ball, he dribbles a few steps before passing it on to the No. 1 player-again in an uncovered place. Both the players continue the practice of passing and receiving the ball in the open space.

Here players practise square passing mixed with passes in open spaces. The No. 2 player, after receiving the pass in the open place, passes the ball to No. 1 with a square pass who, in return, gives a through pass to No. 2.

Passes given to the forwards in the direction shown in broken lines are wrong as the forwards are being marked by the opponents. Passes given through the gaps as shown in the unbroken lines are correct and more profitable. The forwards not only gain the ground but it is also easier for them to make their next move without any interruption.

Through passes to wingers

The left winger should stop the ball with a reverse stick while running when the ball passes much ahead of him. But to receive the ball coming towards his legs he should use the flat side of the stick by keeping it and his body in such a direction that the ball bounces towards the opponent's goal.

To receive feeble passes, the wingers must not wait and should go for the ball without stopping. They should hit towards the centre particularly when they are marked by the opponent.

The right winger should never stop the ball coming from behind, by facing his own goal. Let the ball come in front of him and then only he should stop it in such a way that it goes in the direction in which he has to move.

Cross passes by wingers

Wingers to both the sides move with the ball in speed from the centre-line to the top of the shooting circle and centre towards each other. On their return they practise to reach upto the centre line with minimum impact to the ball to restart exercise.

Crosses made by wingers must be either in level or behind their own positions. After centering the ball, both the wingers must be ready to receive the ball which may come ahead or behind to the level of their positions. This will enable them to control the crosses perfectly.

Inner forwards to receive crosses

The left side player receives the cross from the right-wing whereas the right side player controls the ball coming from his left side. After stopping it, both players shoot at the goal as the situation demand. The crosses far ahead of the shooter and nearer the goal must be converted into a goal with short back swing of the stick and not by hard hits.

Intercepting pass

Here the player No. 1 is Left Back and the No. 2 player is the Right Wing. Both are standing in a diagonal position. The No. 3, Left Half, is about 3 to 4 yards away from the line of hit which is coming from the rival Left Back to his Right wing.

Through the Left Half is not marking the opposing Right wing closely, he is in a good position to intercept the passes given to a player to whom he is responsible to mark.

This practice is not only useful for the player of these positions but every player needs to learn the skill of hitting, stopping and intercepting the hits.

Right-Back, Left wing and Right Half practising

the same skill in a similar fashion given in diagram 41 except that the Right-Half need not to use the reverse stick as he is only intercepting the hits coming from his left side. Therefore it is suggested that the right and left side players should practise the exercises of other side also with the exercise of their own side.

Three players stand on the corner of a triangle with the fourth player inside it. The fourth player endeavours to intercept the pass given by one of the three players. Passes are to be given direct to either of the other two players. One player changes the position with the inside player whose pass is intercepted.

One of the four player in the circle is with the ball. He passes the ball to other players without entering the circle. The players inside the circle intercept the pass. On intercepting the pass or in failing to stop the ball by the outside-players, the middle player changes with the defaulter.

Hitting and stopping by left side players

The left winger practise to stop the ball coming towards him from the hit taken in different directions by the left-Back.

In return left-winger gives practice to stop the ball to his partner, left Back, who changes his position with the side-line in order to receive all hits on his right side.

Shooting at the stump

Eight players with a ball each stand at top of the circle with a radius of 16 yards. They try to knock the stump which is dug in the middle of the circle. To continue the shooting practice, every player is required to get possession of the ball coming in his direction. The player who strikes the stump the highest number of times wins the game. Player fails to stop the incoming short from the opposite direction after fetching the ball goes round the circle with the ball under his control.

The drive will be used in preference to any other stroke when it is necessary to send the ball long distances, to penetrate a rapidly closing gap or to meet a fast-moving player. The value of the drive lies in its versatility. Greatest power is achieved when the head is over the ball at impart, the stick is vertical and the left arm is an extension of the stick handle. A stick which is too long can cause a player to be cramped when the ball is ideally positioned close to the feet, or cause her to make room by pushing the ball further away, leading to a lateral swing of the stick from which the direction is more difficult to control. A high left shoulder over a braced leading leg will keep the ball on line and this is easy to achieve when the swing is in the vertical plane; as the swing becomes more circular excessive rotations are set up in the body which can cause off-balance and a consequent loss of accuracy.

Driving is a linear action. The hands are taken back away from the body into the stroke and the left shoulder holds the swing on line to complete the follow-through. Force can only be applied to the ball during the period of contact which is very short and so the follow-through does not contribute to the speed of the ball, but it does maintain the line of action and aid a balanced recovery. The player should be concerned with the preparatory swing of the stick, which ideally should be short and fast. Because of the limits of stick height imposed by the rules, speed of swing is more important. By taking the hands away from the body the possibility of giving 'sticks' is largely eliminated. The wrists do bend upwards towards the completion of the downward swing and should be encouraged to do so since this whipping movement of the hands, bringing the head of the stick through late, greatly adds to the power of the stroke. At times it will be essential to drive as hard as possible, but most frequently passes require careful judgement of pace as well as direction, particularly when the ball has to be contained in a restricted area. Thus once a player has mastered the shape of the stroke it is important that she plays around with the idea of pace judgement.

Good footwork in the drive will be produced if all the principles mentioned previously are followed. If the feet are to force the hips into the stroke they must be close enough to allow the transfer of weight to take place and must point in the direction and have a lively contact with the ground and readjust their position in a flash lodge in the memory because of their excellent footwork. Ursula Fairbairn and Angela Harrison, who were seen playing for South Africa against England at Wembley Stadium in 1965, were perfect examples of the art of neat footwork.

All these basic points apply to the drive whether it is from a standing position or on the run. Driving a dead ball is generally better accomplished if the ball is played off the left foot, but in the interests of deception a quick pass to the right may be aided by stepping through with the right foot. No such deception is needed when executing an accurate flat hit at a corner., Specialist methods can be used. The striker may stand sideways on to the ball like a golfer, placing both hands together some way down the handle in a 'chopper' grip. A short, crisp, firm swing from the shoulders can be effected or, alternatively, the swing of the stick can be produced entirely by the use of the wrists. In both cases there is no movement of the feet and the body is fairly rigid in order to aid the power and accuracy of the hit. The drive should be player off either foot with ease whether the player is moving slowly or at maximum speed. Too many players need to slow down before hitting. The drive to the left presents fewer difficulties because the left shoulder is already leading the way, but the ball needs to be positioned opposite the left foot to make things easier. Skilled players can execute a perfectly good flat drive to the left with the ball opposite the right foot. The weight is shifted over to that foot and the body is falling away to the right as the ball is struck. Difficult but deceptive, although occasionally resulting in some loss of power.

The drive to the right requires greater bodily adjustments in order to bring the left shoulder round to point in the direction of the intended pass. This brings about a twist in the body while the feet continue running forwards, the ball needs to be behind the rear foot so that the stick can swing freely behind the body. Immediately prior to impact the right foot thrusts through in the line of the hit to take the weight. This necessitates skilful balance and few players seem able to do this at speed. The pass to the right is so often advertised by the sluggish positioning of the feet, the loss of impetus and the prolonged manoeuvre to get the ball in the right place. How frustrating it is to see so many players pull the ball back in order to pass to the right instead of relying on acceleration, twist in the body and dynamic balance.

So far we have suggested how a player can be ideally positioned to execute a drive, but in the game this happy state of affairs does not always exist. It is vital that a player can still make an effective drive when off balance, or having to cope with a bumpy or lust surface, or being pressured by an opponent or running out of space. The reverse stick drive can usefully be employed on occasion to meet such conditions to enable a player to pass to the right or backwards with fewer preliminary adjustments.

Reverse stick play applies whenever the stick is used with the toe of the head pointing in towards the player instead of away. Thus, if the ball is to the left of the player and the state of the game demands that she pass to the right, the stick is reverses, preferably with the toe being turned to the left, and the ball can be driven from left to the right across the body. The same principles apply as in the normal drive although players who experience difficulty in swinging the stick this way may be helped by shortening their gap; that is, taking both hands lower down the handle or placing the hands slightly apart. When the hands are together the left hand predominates, working behind the stick, and if the hands are apart the right hand predominates by pulling the stick through. With the stick reversed the ball can also be passed backwards on the right hand side of the body. Greater power is achieved if the full blade rather than just the toe of the stick meets the ball. Hence, the stick should be vertical.

The push stroke is used when attempting to deceive an opponent by not advertising the bass with a preparation of the stick-in other words when it is necessary to move the ball away quickly to avoid being tackled or to take advantage of an immediate and short-lived opportunity. As suggested, thee is no preparation as the stick is in contact with the ball which is swept away using both hands in unison. The ball is placed level with the front foot and power is added by driving the hips into the stroke off the back foot. Although both hands work in the direction of the push, the left hand acts mainly as the fulcrum for the work of the right hand. To cover a longer distance or increase the speed of the stroke even further the ball can be placed opposite the rear foot, a more sideways stance adopted and the stick can be swept over a greater range. However, with this method the advantage of surprise is frequently lost as a wide base and a static stance normally precede the movement of the ball. Also the leverage is altered as the stick must start further from the body, while the left hand moves the top of the stick backwards before thrusting forwards and initiating the work from the right hand. The push is ideal on fast surfaces where it can be powerful and accurate. Control of pace is generally easier with the push than with the drive as contact with the ball is prolonged and more sensitive.

The fling stroke starts in the same way as the powerful push, but, as well as the contribution made by the body, power is gained by adding a last-minute flick of the wrists and the left achieved by laying the head of the stick back underneath the ball before beginning the forward movement. This stroke should only be used as a pass when the ball is being sent into a space or the spin is turning the ball into the receiver to make close control possible. The stroke can be effected without lift and the ball flicked along the ground spinning as it goes. Either is useful for sending the ball flicked along the ground spinning as it goes. Either is useful for sending the ball between the two opponents to make interception more difficult, and the presence of lift can avoid the disruptive influence of a bad playing surface. Flexibility and whip are the hallmarks of these strokes, and spin can be applied clockwise by wiping the blade of the stick underneath the ball, or anti-clockwise by wiping it up and over the top of the ball. With clockwise spin the ball will tend to hit the ground and kick to the right or hold a straight line, the converse being true when the spin is applied in the opposite direction. Thus when a left half or left inner is passing a forward ball to the left wing clockwise spin will reduce the risk of the ball rolling out of play over the side line. When the ball is played directly to the stick of the left wing anti-clockwise spin will help her to trap the ball on the blade of the stick, as it will be moving towards her.

The scoop stroke is used when height is required as well as length, and this is normally a reverse stick technique in that the ball is played from the left hand side of the body and the grip adjusted so that the stick is used like a shovel. Some players refer to reverse their hand : that is, place the right hand at the top of the handle and the left hand lower down so that the stroke is made to the right of the body. In either case the handle of the stick is lowered to bring the stick from the vertical towards the horizontal with the blade facing upwards. The blade is inserted as far under the ball as possible to establish maximum contact and the body and stick are lifted together.

All these strokes can be used for shooting as well as for passing, but whereas the pass is designed to be easy to receive whenever the situation allows, the shot is used to send the ball past players into the goal. Because of the pressure situation normally pertaining in the circle, a player rarely has a chance to 'set the ball up' for a shot, is less likely to be ideally positioned to make the shot and yet must make every effort to produce an effective attempt at goal. This is where originally and flair can really show themselves, and this is one of the most challenging and exciting aspects of forward play. Generally, successful shots depend on the ball outpacing the opponents, the unexpectedness of the shot or its awkward scored because the ball took an unexpected bounce or deflection. It is most satisfying to score with a brilliant shot, but frequently a weak shot, although not directly effective, may provide a scoring opportunity for another player following up.

Receiving

In free play the prerequisite for a good pass is control of both moving the ball coming in to a player. The ball can be hit first time so that the pass is really a redirection of the approaching ball, frequently with the addition of some pace to speed up the quick passing movement between two players used to eliminated an opponent or take immediate advantage of a diminishing space. When needing to collect the ball and hold it on the stick without fear of harassment, all players should be prepared to make space in order to receive it either by meeting the ball or dropping away from an opponent before the ball is passed. The full blade of the stick should be turned to face the approaching ball and the stick should be on the ground ready to lift and gather the ball which pops up unexpectedly. The stick should be considered to be a magnet attracting the ball to it and a relaxed grip will help to cushion the ball on impact and hold it in close to the stick. Lively footwork will make repositioning easier. It may help a player to try to watch the ball right on to the stick. To actually do so is extremely difficult, and in reasonable conditions the skilled player will have directed her attention elsewhere before contact is made.

When wishing to stop the ball dead, the right hand may be lowered down the handle to give close support to the blade of the stick as the ball is contacted. This more static method of receiving is used primarily at corners and by defenders fielding a hard ball coming straight towards them. Attacking players in free play tend to develop a more fluid type of receiving, frequently swerving as the ball it taken to switch the direction of the attack or avoid the ball's being intercepted. Receiving is one of the most crucial elements of technique and it should be stressed that it is fundamental to successful play because all that is to follow is dependent upon immediate, close control of the approaching ball.

Good receiving is epitomized by the perfectly timed interception which enables a player moving at speed to collect and move away with the ball under absolute control. Precise anticipation is required to ensure contact with the ball and different methods may be employed depending upon the angle and speed at which the ball is moving and the position of the intercepting player and her speed to the ball. When moving fairly slowly and when taking small steps it is possible to stop quickly and turn the blade of the stick to trap the speed or wishes to avoid a tackle the blade of the stick may point in the direction of her travel so that as the ball comes across it is deflected into her pathway enabling her to maintain her speed.

Every player can envisage the times that a ball comes towards her bobbing about and deviating from its line, and frequently when there is plenty of time to cope with the approaching ball doubts flood into the mind and by the time it arrives the player has convinced herself that she is going to miss it. Sure enough those doubts become certainties and the ball scuttles by to continue merrily on its way. Good receiving is assisted by a positive attitude.

Although the practice is not extensively, the ball can be received in the hand. If taken in the air, it may be caught or cushioned by the hand but it must drop vertically from the point of contact. On the ground the ball is usually caught in the hand by having the fingers spread close to the ground so that the ball can be clasped momentarily to prevent any rebound. The hand can be placed with the wrist nearest to the ground so that the fingers close over the top of the ball, but there is more chance of the ball bouncing away and the receiver has to crouch near the ground, thereby restricting any movements she might need to make should the ball deviate from its line of approach. A player may stop the ball with her hand and play it herself, but most frequently this is a combined operation between two players. The receiver must stop the ball without her body being in the way of the striker. As this is most frequently used at corners it can be seen that having the ball hit from the left enables the receiver to keep her body out of the way. It is possible to do this from the right if the receiver has her back to the hitter with her fingers touching the ground and having stopped the ball she sways back to allow the striker a clear view of it. The ball must be stopped dead and a great deal of practice is required to perfect this technique.

How the ball is received will depend largely upon the subsequent actions which need to follow the collection of the ball. It is obviously easier to face the incoming ball, but this is rarely possible or indeed advisable in hockey for two reasons. Firstly, a player hardly ever wishes to send the ball straight back to its original starting point and so the feet should be organized towards the preparation for the next action at it is received and, secondly, a player will always try to collect the ball facing the goal she is attacking to avoid the possibility of obstruction. Bearing those points in mind we will assume that the player is always making the effort to face her attacking goal, wherever the ball is coming from, and we will note how the technique changes according to the direction from which the ball approaches.

The following point should apply each time the ball is received :

(a) Feet pointing towards the attacking goal or at least having the intention of moving in that direction.

(b) Feet already moving, therefore ready to make a large or fine adjustment very quickly;

(c) Right hand placed lower than usual down the handle for greater control;

(d) Blade of the stick facing the incoming ball;

(e) Tension of grip release on contact.

To take a ball approaching from the right of the body the shoulders have to twist and the left arm reach away from the body to bring the full face of the stick to the ball. When the ball is coming in more from behind the receiver the excessive body twist can be eliminated by reversing the stick to trap the ball before resuming the normal playing position. The orthodox method used in this situation causes the ball to be collected behind the feet which is undesirable. Whenever receiving a ball coming in from behind it is essential that the player moves laterally to one side or the other so that she is not directly in line with the ball. It is then possible to bring the ball forward quickly to the front of the body instead of having it stuck behind the heels. For a ball approaching from the left the receiver will need either to let the ball cross in front of the body or move the feet inside the ball. A ball travelling straight towards a player should be taken well in front of the feet providing space for manoeuvre. Little readjustment should be needed when a pass is sent to a player as it should be accurate, but obviously not all passes are perfect. A sudden acceleration will frequently be required to enable a player to position most appropriately for receiving a particular pass and for a bad pass or an interception the reach may need to be extended by temporarily removing the right hand from the stick. There are two occasions when reversing the stick is of great advantage: for the ball travelling from right to left in front of a player where the feet cannot speed up sufficiently to get behind the ball and for the ball sent to the non-stick side of an approaching player.

Planner progressive practices for stickwork

Because there are several books composed entirely of practices it is intended here only to give examples of how the degree of difficulty can be developed. It is not envisaged that each stage suggested should be undertaken by all players. For accomplished players it may be wise to move from very basic practices to pressure practices to see if the technique has been retained. Such players will need to keep returning to the practice of basic techniques in their simplest form from time to time. The drive has been chosen to show how a technique can be taken through from the simplest level to the most complex. Throughout we assume that the technique does not have to be learned, merely reinforced.

1. One ball to each player. Drive into a space; chase; collect; repeat. Coaching points: look for the next space before reaching the ball. Approach the ball ready to drive in the chosen direction. Keep the ball moving as you collect and prepare drive. Short, quick backlift...feet continually adjusting...head over the ball at impact. Vary the distance of the hit. Exaggerate the follow-through to smooth out the stroke, and have the weight of the body travelling through the drive.

2. Three players and one ball. Concentrated practice in driving to the right and to the left with the players positioned in a triangle. The ball must be sent directly to each player.

   Coaching points: the receiver has to move to meet the ball, adjusting her feet ready for the next pass which will of course be in a different direction. Actual possession of the ball should be for as short a time as possible. Triangular formation should be retained.

3. Two players and one ball. Passing to a moving player so that ball and stick meet each other at exactly the right moment. Coaching points: look to see where the receiver is asking for the ball. Judge pace and direction. Adjust speed of swing to allow for this. Reposition immediately to become the receiver. Note well that the receiver should neither need to hesitate in her running nor have to chase the ball. The recipient can vary where she asks for the ball by presenting the blade of her stick to the sender, and she can vary the speed at which she begins her movement for the ball.

4. Two players each with five balls positioned side by side and about 5½ yd. from restraining line. Driving for distance at speed. The first ball to be driven on the run before crossing the line and the distance it travels noted. Each player quickly returns to the start to repeat the activity and this continues until all the balls have been used. Award three points to the player whole ball travelled the longest distance and two points to the player who finished first.

5. Four players and one ball. Specific practice for hard drives hit square to the left and right. Player A feed player B who dribbles 5 yd. and passes right to C who collects and feeds the ball to D. All players turn to face the opposite direction and the practice is repeated. A and B, C and D can change roles the practice can be returned round to make the hard drive to the left instead of the right.

6. Three attackers spread across the field with a defender approaching the central player and the ball in possession of one of the outer attackers. The defender approaches as the central player receives a pass following which she must pass before the defender can interfere and both outer attackers must accelerate forwards asking for the ball. The central player can select which one to use. The ball must be played on to the stick of the accelerating player. The practice is resumed by turning to play in the opposite direction, moving each player on one place after several turns. Pressure can be lessened or increased by varying the distance the defender has to cover the forward centrally placed.

7. When receiving at a corner the source of the ball and the target are know and some preliminary preparations can be made. From whichever side the corner is taken the receiver should have her feet pointing towards the goal and not the hitter. Then if the ball is hit accurately precious time will not be wasted while the feet are moved to shoot. From the right the ball must be taken by the left foot for an immediate shot to be possible. From the left the ball must be allowed to travel across the body before shooting. This can be practised until the player shooting does not even need to look up and check on the angle of her shot. She should be able to keep her head down throughout the reception and shot. Pressure can be increased by introducing a third player to rush the receiving forward.

8. Pressure practice. Two players, each with a ball, facing each other approximately 15—20 yd. apart. Rule: the ball must be controlled before being

driven. Both players start together and the aim is that each player intends that the other shall have to cope with two balls simultaneously.

Stealing

Possession can be gained from the bully, from intercepting or by dispossessing the opponent directly by tackling her. The last is one of the more difficult facets of the game to practice because it cannot be done alone. Essentially there is a need to learn the timing of the tackle. Even when a partner is provided for the practice she can either try to help too much by making it easy or she can ruin it by making the manoeuvre too difficult too soon.

That specialist activity, the bully, where two players without interference from others are given an equal chance of winning the ball should not deteriorate into a tackle. The skill of successful bullying lies in stealing the ball before the opponent can touch it. Only when the two players involved arrive with their sticks on the ball at the same time should tackling become necessary. Various ploys are tried in order to gain an advantage at the bully and it has to be admitted that those who have a number of tricks up their sleeves are the successful ones. When meeting such an expert it is wise to be alert and make the first two movements with the stick slowly and fairly high above the ball but make the last touch very quick and close to the ball. Do not be lulled into a sense of false security. Beware the strong player who may knock away your stick vigorously on the third tap to delay your movements to the ball, or the player who hooks her stick on the third movement to block your access to the ball. Though this is a foul it may be done too quickly to be noticed by the most astute umpire. Within the framework of the rules the following methods may be tried at the bully: pulling the ball to the left to pass it or to travel with it; reversing the stick to send the ball back to the supporting defender; pushing the ball between the opponent's feet can be rather negative at it frequently leads to obstruction by that opponent, which will stop the flow of an attack even if the free hit is awarded.

Choose the method you intend to use before taking up your stance and make sure the ball is not sitting in a hole. Place it on the highest bit of ground available so that you can make maximum contact with the surface of the ball. For the pull to the left have the feet a little further from the ball, still allowing the arms to be flexed for the snatching action to follow. When the ball is pulled away the left foot can step aside allowing an immediate push pass to be made ahead of the left inner. When pushing to the right stand closer to the ball so that stronger leverage is possible. In addition it may help if the right hand is placed further down the stick. Knowing which method you intend to use, on the third movement of the bully the stick head must be manipulated to meed the ball correctly. This has to be done very quickly, especially if this is to be reversed for a backward pass. Look out for subtle innovations. Be alert, quick and on your toes ready to move. If you win the bully, remember to be quick off the mark with either a pass or a rapid dribble away from the area.

The playing position largely dictates the types of tackle that will be used most frequently. A fullback or sweeper usually meets an opponent coming straight towards her with the ball. She is able to choose her ground, decide whether to hold her position or advance to meet her opponent. This decision is affected by the related positions of her team-mates and the proximity of the circle edge and the goal. She may, by her positioning, for her opponent to try to pass her on one side rather than the other, thereby preventing her from using her preferred method of dodging. The defender will be on the alert to sense any momentary loss of control on the part of the attacker and time her tackle accordingly. A resilient stance will allow the defender to pounce quickly and reposition in the event of a missed tackle. Firmness in the tackle is essential if the ball is to be won. If a player is beaten or the ball is placed behind her for an opponent to run on to she will have to turn to make a chasing tackle from behind the retreating opponent. This also applies to forwards who run back to harass their opponents. Such tackles usually have to be made while both players are running at speed. Because of the tactical commitments the chasing player is not always free to decide on the side from which she will make the tackle. Wing halves, for example, when chasing their opposing wings will need to tackle from the goal side. This means the left half must become highly skilled at the more difficult tackle from the non-stick side while the right half has an easier task. Slow positioning or a speedy opponent may cause the initiation of the tackle with only the left hand on the stick to extend the reach. Such a measure may enable the tackler to place her second hand on the stick and assume greater strength and control. Being able to run at speed and yet take small steps is an asset. Those players who take long, lunging, despairing strides will find themselves stranded if they miss the ball at the first attempt. The aim in tackling should always be to gain possession and not merely to spoil the progress of the opponent.

In all tackling the eye should be on the ball and on the feet of the opponent to anticipate any change of pace direction which might be made. The stick should be scraping the ground as the player approaches the ball.

The straight tackle requires the player tackling to move in towards the stick side of her opponent and, in order to time the tackle correctly, she must be prepared to sway from one foot to the other very rapidly. This may even cause the attacker to lose control by distracting her attention. She may also vary the pace of her approach provided she is taking small steps to maintain her balance and facilitate immediate acceleration in any direction. The defender must not commit herself so fully to the tackle that she cannot keep control of the ball if successful, or turn to tackle again if beaten. When the approaching forward has good control then pretending to tackle can benefit the defender. Swaying her hips can cause the forward to respond to what she assumes to be a committed movement by the defender. Because the latter has retained her balance and anticipated the response she can move quickly to tackle the opponent unexpectedly. Normally in a straight tackle the hands will be apart and the stick. Sometimes a jab may precede the two handed tackle if the ball runs loose for a moment. A well timed backward step may provide additional space and time for the defender to make an effective tackle. Such a move may cause the attacker to change her mind. Causing the attacker to be indecisive is the first stage of making a successful tackle. In this particular one-versus-one encounter the player who first notices the change of weight from one foot to the other and adapts her movement accordingly is likely to win the ball.

Stick-side tackles from behind should be easy to master provided that the tackling player leaves sufficient space between herself and her opponent. As the stick is swung close to the ground the blade should be facing the goal into which the tackling player is shooting. When the stick makes contact with the ball the feet should continue their running until the player is facing her opponent. This enables her to put all her weight behind her stick when the final stages of the tackle are made. If she cannot gain so much ground, the tackling player can remove her right hand from her stick to give herself extra reach as she sweeps the stick in an arc parallel to the ground to contact the ball, either to knock it gently to the side or to trap it against her opponent's stick until she has time to place herself behind the ball and complete the tackle.

Tackling from the non-stick side of a player presents more problems since the tackle has to be made across the body of the player in possession. Numerous methods have been devised which enable contact to be made with the ball without causing bodily contact with the player in possession or obstruction of her progress. Six useful tackles are described here.

(a) The circular tackle: the tackling player keeps two hands on her stick, runs ahead of her opponent, turns to face her and draws the ball away as she continues to run round to the stick side of the opponent.

(b) The jab tackle: the tackle player keeps only the left or the right hand on her stick, the blade of which faces upwards. The stick is jabbed across in front of the player in possession to know the ball away from her stick. The tackling player must either follow her jabbing action by running round and ahead of her opponent, keeping a good distance between the two of them, to collect the ball or she must rapidly withdraw her stick from the ball, allowing the opponent to run on, and then retrieve it. The method of completing the tackle selected will depend on the forward speed of the opponent to be robbed.

(c) The reverse stick tap tackle: the player about to tackle has the left hand at the top of the stick which has its toe facing the ground. She reaches across the opponent and taps the ball away to the far side. The ball is collected after the opponent has run on. The advantage of this technique is that it allows the ball to be played earlier and gives the opponent less warning.

(d) The reverse stick check is very similar to the above except that the ball is stopped dead rather than being knocked away. The grip of the tackling player needs to be particularly firm as her stick may need to withstand the pressure of the opponent's stick on the ball momentarily, before removing her stick quickly from the pathway of the running opponent.

(e) The reverse stick pull with one hand: instead of simply checking the ball possession is gained sooner by the ball being pulled diagonally backwards towards the tackling player. In the three previous tackles described the tackle can be initiated from behind but in all cases the right shoulder has to be pulled back away from the opponent to avoid obstruction. In this tackle the tackling player needs to be at least level with her opponent as she turns towards her. The ball can then be drawn away towards the tackling player who is already facing her attacking goal and ready to move off with the ball.

(f) The reverse stick pull with two hands is very similar to the previous tackle but the second hand remains on the stick to add more power to the action of drawing the ball away. The disadvantage of this is that the tackler needs to get slightly ahead of the opponent before initiating the tackle.

Practices for tackling

1. The straight tackle. Two players and one ball. At a reasonable speed the player in possession takes the ball towards a goal area and the defender approaches trying to remove the ball to prevent the attacker from scoring.

   Coaching points: defender watches feet of attacker and the ball simultaneously with both hands on her stick and her stick on the ground. The blade of her stick should be facing the ball-balanced and mobile. The defender has got to have a realistic situation with the attacker being allowed to try and pass her in variety of ways to keep her guessing as to what is going to happen and when. The practice she needs is of timing and judgement.

   2a. Chasing tackles from the non-stick side. One player with the ball sends the ball ahead.

Keeping the ball on the right, chase it, go beyond it and then turn in to face it before touching it with the stick. Return to line of running and repeat. Aim to leave as short a time as possible between sending the ball away and touching it again.

Coaching points: begin the turn of the shoulders before getting level with the ball. Make sure the step which leads into the turn is on the right foot which should be ahead of the ball and across its line of travel. Pivot around the right foot to swing the hips through, following the lead given by the left shoulder.

2b. Three players with one ball. Player A sends the ball ahead and runs after it. Player B starts one stride ahead of A and chases the ball too. Player C positions to receive a pass from B in the event of her getting the ball first. The points mentioned in the previous practice apply. In addition player B, the tackling player, has to adjust her distance from a player A to prevent body contact as each is chasing the ball.

Additional coaching points: put the stick to the ball as early as possible and wrap it round the ball as the feet body pivot. Move the ball out of line of the stick of the incoming player. In order to steal time a tackling player who is unable to get ahead of her opponent can use the jab before completing the tackle.

3. The practices are made more difficult by the attacker starting with the ball in her close possession and having the freedom to swerve either way or the freedom to pass. The tackling player

then needs to assess whether the player in possession intends to continue or to pass in order to judge the timing of her tackle. At this point the various forms of reverse stick tackle can be practised.

4a. Chasing tackles from the stick side. In the first practice the same procedure can be adopted as for tackles from the non-stick side.

Coaching points: chase with the ball on the left. Put the stick on to the ball and ahead of it as early as possible. Keep the feet running rapidly to get the weight behind the stick with the body facing the attacking goal.

4b. Three players and one ball. Player A sets off with the ball and two strides later player B chases on the stick side, completes the tackle and passes to player C. It is possible to do this practice with only two players so that the tackler must accelerate away from her opponent who immediately turns to give chase and tackles back. This can continue as long as the stamina of the two players lasts. On occasions it may not be possible to reach the ball with two hands on the stick. In this instance the left hand lunge initiates the tackle.

Coaching points: keep two hands on the stick for as long as possible. Keep a good distance away from the body of the attacker to avoid the possibility of playing her stick instead of the ball.

Evasion

There will be many occasions during a game when a

player will need to evade being tackled or meet other players and take the ball past them. For this skill to develop, close ball control is required, coupled with the ability to change pace and direction rapidly. Ideally, then, the essentials for evading should be introduced in the early stage of learning top travel with the ball. Swerving, checking, accelerating and sidestepping can be practised alone with or without the presence of obstacles. However, inanimate objects do not respond and although it might be easy to learn to dribble around stationary objects, true evasion can only occur when another player is involved. A battle of wits can develop which is just as real as the techniques which are exercised.

A successful dodge requires less space and the attacker has possession of the ball immediately after passing her opponent. The secret for success lies not only in the close control, which is essential, but in the production of acceleration at exactly the right moment. For this acceleration to available an opponent should never be approached at maximum speed. There should always be something left in reserve. The dodge must not be advertised and the attacker should get as close to defender as possible before initiating the movement. When taking the ball to the left a preliminary movement to the right may throw the opponent on to the wrong foot and so allow the dodge to be completed. If the defender is not tempted to accept the bait the initial movement to the right can be continued and a successful dodge accomplished. A feint with stick or body may draw the defender into committing herself, so providing a route to get past her.

If players experience difficulty, it may necessary to

isolate a type of dodge and practise this separately. Here are a few recognized examples, but remember that successful evasion may involve a combination of these actions:

Left dodge: the left foot steps square to the left providing room for the ball top be pulled across after it, before accelerating forwards past the defender. If the defender anticipates and reaches out to tackle, the ball can be slipped between her stick and right foot instead of being taken all the way round on the outside.

Nutcracker: by forcing defender to move sideways, the ball can be sent between her feet and retrieved on the far side. Contact with the ball should be lost for the shortest possible time.

Right dodge: as above, but the ball is played to the non-stick side of the player.

Scoop dodge: the ball can be lifted slightly over the top of the stick of an opponent. This is difficult to do without advertising the intention.

Reverse stick dodge: the same as the pull to the left but in reverse. This time the right foot leads the way with a side step and with the stick reversed the ball is dragged to the right and then taken through on the non-stick side of the defender.

Stop-go: a change of pace may provide the opportunity to accelerate past a defender who has been caught unawares by the sudden change of speed.

A defender may also use a dodge to make more space for her clearance, and every player has at times to avoid being tackled while waiting for an opportune moment to pass the ball.

Practices for evading

1. Each player has a ball. Keeping the ball on the stick, swerve, check, change direction and change pace in a confined space-for example, the 25 yd. area or the goal circle.

   Coaching points: be constantly aware of others to be avoided. Feel the pressure of the ball on the stick all the time. Emphasize sudden sharp moments of acceleration without losing control. Have the stick vertical and kept well away from the body.

2. As above, but three player out of the twenty or so to have no ball at all. Those without a ball aim to acquire one without breaking any hockey rules. This adds extra pressure because any player in possession has to head for spaces and at the same time be aware of several rapidly changing opponents appearing out of the blue.

3. Two versus one-the two starting in possession of the ball. The defender chooses to mark one of the two players. The marked player may choose to dodge or pass but the free forward may not travel with the ball and must receive and pass immediately. Their aim is to get past the defender and score. So some target must be provided for this.

   Coaching points: watch the feet of the defender to see where her weight is committed. Keep the ball close to the stick. Be ready to accelerate into and out of the dodge. Be aware of whether the defender is trying to cut of the pass too. Judge the distance from the defender before dodging or passing, aiming to find the last possible effective moment.

4. Practice to enforce collection and control of the ball immediately following a dodge. One player with a ball starts about II yd. away from two defenders who are positioned one behind the other, as in covering, and some 7½yd. apart. The second defender may not approach the attacker until the ball has passed the first defender. The attacker aims to have sufficient control of the ball following the first dodge to enable her to evade the second defender. A lateral restriction of 5 yd. can be applied to made it even more difficult. The nature of the second dodge is dependent upon where and how the first dodge is completed.

Goalkeeping

The unique position of the goalkeeper necessitates an additional set of techniques using the legs and feet in ways similar in principle to those described using a stick. She has to receive the ball either by stopping or redirecting it; to send the ball away as a pass; to dispossess an opponent by tackling. A highly skilled goalkeeper will be seen to stop a straight shot by flexing the knees and ankles to cushion the impact of the ball and then, using either feet or stick, move with the ball to secure a better angle for her clearance. This manoeuvre is only possible if she is well balanced with the weight on the balls of the feet and the shoulders forward. Should the ball rebound it may be drawn back with the stick nearer to the feet before being dispatched, leaving very few chances for any poaching forward to snap up.

The goalkeeper frequently finds herself in a quick-reflex situation where she does well to get her foot to the ball and prevent a goal from being scored. In such cases the ball can fly off the foot and back into play. By placing her foot firmly at the appropriate angle to the ball she may be able to deflect it constructively.

Just as the blade of the stick can be exploited and send the ball in different ways so can the kicking foot. For greater accuracy and to offer the best chance of making a flat kick the instep (or more precisely, the base of the big toe) is used in a sweeping action to finish with the weight on that kicking foot. When a shot is coming in flat and fast a stab kick can be used. This has no follow-through because the foot is used to dig into the ground immediately in line with the ball presenting a wall to reverse its direction. In fact the original pace of the ball is being used in the clearance rather than the strength of the goalkeeper.

One advanced technique used by very experienced goalkeepers is that of kicking across the line of the ball using the outer border of the foot, following through with a fairly high knee-lift. This causes the ball to spin off in a direction not expected by the incoming opposing forwards. Kicking on the volley or half-volley can be used to give greater power to the clearance. Usually this kick is seen when the goalkeeper has had to hand-stop a lifted ball which is then dropped vertically either on to the top of the front part of the foot or on to the ground to be struck by the same part of the foot just as the ball begins to rise. For balance and ball control the knee of the kicking leg needs to be lifted high and turned inwards. Since use of the hand has arisen it might be wise to consider how a goalkeeper can turn his necessary action to advantage. She is not penalized if the ball does not drop vertically, though she cannot propel it forwards.

This gives her some scope for arranging deliberately where the ball shall drop. Though she cannot place the ball the goalkeeper can determine whether her hand is close or far away from her body when it makes contact with the ball; whether her body has turned before the contact is made; whether she catches and drops or uses the palm of the hand as a rebound surface.

The goalkeeper has to be particularly agile when moving out to meet a lone forward in possession. Though she has to cover the ground quickly, she must arrive close to that forward sufficiently balanced to be in a good position for tackling. As she gets closer to the opponent so her strides should shorten until she is ready to pause, posed with pads together, ready to move into a tackle with either foot. A firm thrust, getting the instep against the ball, is the most effective way of robbing the opponent.

Goalkeeping is a highly individual task in which each player develops her own idiosyncrasies. The type of kicker and leg-pad preferred by her may influence the adaptations she makes to the basic techniques. The solid hoof-type of kicker while giving good protection to the foot tends to be clumsy and to impair accuracy of kicking. Canvas kickers seem to be preferred for their lightness and their ability to mould to the foot. To increase their powers of protection additional material can be inserted to meet the special requirement of the individual. The greatest variations in style seem to stem from the part of the foot preferred for kicking by a goalkeeper. Her preferences will lead her to adapt techniques for her own use.

The lifting of kicks is not to be encouraged because of the proximity of other players unless great control can be exercised. Generally the goalkeeper will be seeking to direct the ball through a gap in the crowded circle or on to the stick of a free colleague who might have more time and a better opening for clearing.

An individual approach to skill

Top-class players may well refine the basic techniques to suit their own requirements. Some may be idiosyncratic, others may be ostentatious, but many are clever personal adaptations which often prove particularly effective. Selecting examples is difficult because such refinements are so subtle that an observer needs to be close to discern them. They would not necessarily be obvious to a spectator and therefore we have been forced into choosing examples which were encountered through playing with the people concerned.

For example, Denise Parry would bemuse defenders by the use of her stick in the left hand only. The ball would seem to be out of reach and the defender, sensing this, would move in to intercept only to find that Denise had flashed out her stick like a snake's tongue to steer the ball away from the defender's stick. Then she would slide past with the ball under absolute control. Left wings on executing a feint to the left round the opposing halfback usually have to move away a few steps before being able to centre the ball. Not so Melvyn (Hickey) Pignon. She would swerve much further with her body so that it zoomed ahead of the ball and at the completion of the dodge a quick lift of the stick would send the ball streaking across the field to the delight of the waiting forwards. Backs, being approached by a forward who has control of the ball, have been known to hold the stick vertically and move it rapidly left and right in front of their feet. Many forwards have been mesmerized by this and found the defender calmly removing the ball from them.

All these players devised the technical adaptations to increase their own effectiveness in their own particular playing circumstances. Ultimately each player must be responsible for doing this for herself. She must also continue to increase the range of her technical skills. In this way she will be able to meet the demands made on her and counter the advance knowledge that some teams may have of her play. There is a temptation, having reached top levels of play, for players to reject the need to practise stickwork regularly. It is at this point in a player's career that she should seek to be absolute master of ball and stick and be able to use her skills faster and more precisely than anyone else. To be outwitted is not to be disgraced, but to be beaten by superior skill hurts. It should stimulate the player to work hard to eliminate any deficiencies which have been identified. The basic techniques must be practised under pressure in order to retain their sharpness and at the same time help to keep the player fit enough to be in the right place at the right time to use these skills to best advantage. A high level of skills gives a player freedom. Freedom to choose what to do, when to do it and how to do it-all of which adds to the enjoyment of the game.

3

HOW TO PLAY HOCKEY

Goal-keeper

The goalkeeper fills one of the key positions in the team. He is the last line of defence and a match may be won or lost by his actions. The first essential for a goalkeeper is to have the proper equipment. He should play with a stick best suited to him and should wear pads and kickers which give adequate protection and fit the legs and feet in such a way that they do not hamper his movements. As regards the hand glove, it is a matter of personal taste.

Qualities. The secret of good goalkeeping is clever anticipation, courage, alertness, good judgement in coming out of goal, keen eyesight and presence of mind. Anticipation plays an important part in the make-up of a first class goalkeeper. To grasp this art I would advice goalkeepers to play in different positions, particularly in the forward line, in some practice games. The goalkeeper must also perfect the art of stopping the ball in such a way that it does not rebound out of his control. Always alert, his eyes should be fixed on the ball and opponent's stick and he should be ever ready to meet a sudden attack. He must not be disheartened or lose his head if he is beaten, but instead, he should be prepared to save more goals being scored against him.

Positional play and clearances. The goalkeeper should never be stationary, he should move from side to side of the goal according to the position of the ball in the field in order to keep himself alert and to be in the correct position if the attack develops. He must understand the difference between taking position just on the goal-line and the advantage of moving about a yard or so ahead of it. In the former case the opposing forward has no easier chance to take a shot on either side of the goalkeeper but in the latter position the goalkeeper has narrowed the angle. Another advantage would be of being in a better position of having a second chance of clearing the ball which spins off the pads and drops behind. In addition to this, there will be less distance to go out in case he decides to tackle the oncoming forward. Many goalkeepers make a mark to show the middle of the goal to facilitate positioning.

The goalkeeper to come out of the goal, must work in harmony with the other members of the defence especially the full backs and centre half. He should never leave to goal if one of the defence members is in a position to tackle the oncoming forward. If situation demands, run fast and go all out to charge. Supposing the centre forward is dashing on alone and the back is not in a position to tackle him just on the top of the circle. This will hamper and delay the progress of the centre forward and in the meanwhile the back may have time to cover the vacant goal. In clearing; it is wiser to send the ball to the sides than down the centre.

Exercises. (1) Two goalkeepers can practice by kicking the ball with either foot to each other. (2) Kick the ball hard against the wall and learn to stop with either foot and kick on the rebound, keeping your weight forward with the ball underneath your face. (3) Play out in the field in different positions as often as you can to have a general idea of the game (4) Ran and dribble with pads on.

The following points should be noted carefully:

1. It is a bad habit to talk to the spectators.
2. Never treat shots, even feeble ones, as easy and always stop first and then kick.
3. Do not close your eyes when a quick shot comes towards you; neither should you turn your back or side to stop it.
4. Never bring your stick higher than your shoulders to stop the ball in the air, as this may result in a penalty corner or a penalty stroke.
5. Never propel, push, or throw the ball with your hand or chest. This infringement means a penalty stroke.
6. Never interfere or play in the game without having your own stick in your hand.
7. Do not sit on the ball.
8. Avoid unnecessary obstruction.
9. Never stop the ball which is harmlessly going out of the field.
10. Never clear the ball to the centre of the field.
11. Avoid using your pads and boots outside the striking circle.
12. Never the stationary while in the goal.

13. Never leave the goal unless it is absolutely essential to do so.

He must watch the progress of the game even when the game is going on in the opponent's half and should be ready to put himself in the game when a sudden counter attack takes place. He should also make himself useful by giving instructions to his defence and warn his players not to indulge in wrong tactics.

Full backs. The full back who would like to be in the right position at the right time can never get a single minute to relax himself. If his forwards are in the attack on the right side the right back position should be on the centre line and the left back, covering his partner, would be near the twenty five yards line. If the game suddenly changes or develops on the left side then both the backs would interchange with each other. In the absence of his wing half his job is to meet the opposite winger. Finally the most important thing for the backs to do is to move up at once after releasing the pressure of the game from their own half to cover the field as much as the progress of the game permits. This will not only avoid any gap but will also enable to back to be in an advance position to put the ball in re-attack when he would intercept the ball from the counter attack. The back holding a right position would always be available to take a free hit himself in his own half and would give an opportunity to his half backs to take up the positions in the level of opponent forwards to give way to the ball towards their forwards. The full-back who never relaxes can also prove himself a great back taking up a right position to receive the ball from push-in particularly when both the attacking players to left wing are covered by the opponents. Playing up and down, covering each other according to the position of the ball and trying to anticipate the next move of the game will keep the full-backs busy all the time of play.

Half backs. The position of the centre half, who has to cover the middle of the field, is such that he can never dream of taking a rest for a second. The centre half who is found behind as a third full back when the ball is away from him and with his attackers is not justifying his job. He should always move up with his forwards and if the attack is developed from the wing, his right position is behind that wing half who would be in attacking position just behind his forwards.

Wing halves are the link between defence and attack. Their duty is to tackle the opposing winger forwards as well as to feed their forwards. This shows that the wing halves play a vital part both in attack and defence, who would naturally be moving up and down with the game. When the ball is in action on the right wing, the left half, in this case should not think that he has to do nothing. His duty is to leave his opposing winger to keep himself ready to mark the opposite inside forward and to take such a position on the field that will enable him to get back to help his defence when his team's attack breaks down. Secondly all the halves should keep themselves in move to cover each other either in diagnol position when the ball is in attack in one of the wings or in triangular position when the attack is from the middle of the field. The most salient point for the defence is to move up at once to their proper positions instead of remaining in defensive position when the ball is driven hard from their own half into the opponent's half.

Forwards. Many old veterans hold the opinion with which I also fully agree and that is that the team which has two working inside forwards and two wing halves of the same calibre, is surely built on a very strong footings. The players of both the positions should always be on the move. The inside forwards should at once come back to help their defence when their team's attack breaks down. The remaining forwards also should come back upto the centre line in the first instance and then gradually move towards their goal. It is often seen that the off day of a good winger is compassed by making him unable to move in attack by his opponent wing half or by failing to feed him properly by his team mates. In such cases instead of feeling himself out of the game he should put himself in the game either by disturbing the play of his opponent forward or by tackling the opponent half of his side. These tactics which may look destructive will certainly bring him in the game and would justify his inclusion in the team. This surely means that a player who has once entered into the field of play can not afford to relax. He has to keep himself in the game all the time regardless of whether the game is on or off in his playing distance. The good player who is away from the game may ask himself, "Am I doing something for my team"? The apt answer to this monologue will make him realise his job.

Push-in

Players responsible for taking the push-in should practise to push the ball along the ground. Long and fast pushes along the side-line is more profitable than giving a risky pass to the closer team-mate when it is to be taken within an area of 16 yards of the players who pushes-in

Push-in within the area covered by the striking circle of opposite team should be taken by the wingers, instead of the defenders, and it is more advantageous if it is taken towards the circle. To receive or to black the push-in, the players should make themselves available near the spot of the occurrence but not within the distance of five yards from the ball. The direction of push-in in which it should be made when they are taken within the area of (i) own 16 yards (ii) mid field and (iii) opponent's 16 yards.

Bully-off

To start the game the bully-off takes place at the middle of the centre-line by two rival players. The grip of the two players is more or less similar to the one when the players take the push. Both these players stand square facing the side lines. The players strike their sticks three times over the ball and without disturbing it. Before striking the stick of each other they must touch the ground first. After the three taps either of the player can play the ball.

To success at the bully-off gives an initial advantage of developing the attack in a very first minute of game—on many occasions this has resulted in a good lead to the team. To win the bully the following are the usual tactics and the players are advised to practice them:

1. Draw the ball towards the feet and flick or push it to one of your team-mates.
2. Flick and ball back to the centre-half, positioned behind the ball, with the reverse stick.
3. Pull the ball slightly backwards with the reverse stick and push it to one of the forwards.

One of the players who takes the bully after completing it passes the ball to his half-back who starts the attack for his team through the right-winger.

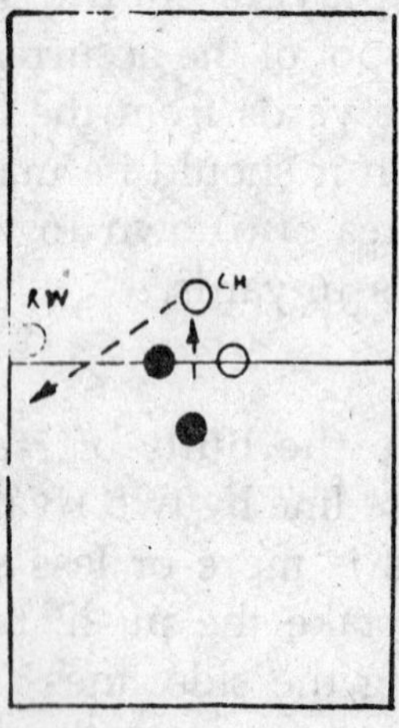

Rule-makers are now thinking of replacing the centre-bully with simple pass backward.

Dribbling with abrupt change

Players at the top of the circle move the ball in control first clockwise and then anticlockwise. A player found without the ball at the signal of the trainer losses a point. While changing the direction the players must face towards the circle. If the players are more, they may also be arranged inside the circle to do the same practice.

Dribbling and passing

In a small circle one ball is placed for each team, consisting of four players, lined up outside the big circle. On signal the No. 1 players of both the teams run for the ball to push it from inside the small circle to their No. 2 player to complete the circle. The ball is to be received and after completing the circle it must be returned within the restricted area. The No. 3 player after completing the practice replaces the No. 1 player to complete the game.

The player whose ball reaches in the small circle first wins the game.

Ball control and measured passes

Eight players are divided into two group. No. 1 to 4 and 9 to 12 are with the ball. No. 1 moves with the ball upto some distance before passing the ball with reverse flick towards his opposite player No. 5. Before returning the ball with flat side of the stick, No. 5 should also move some distance. His pass must be much ahead and within reach of player No. 1. The practice continues in a similar fashion upto the fixed distance. While returning to the starting point, No. 5 uses the reverse flick and 1 the right side flick. The practice continues till all the players take their turn.

Like other practices, it should also be done in a competitive manner, to create more interest, with other group or group. The group which completes the exercise first is the winner.

Ball in close contact

A player carries the ball to his left side and after the third tap brings the ball to his right side with a reverse stick to move ahead. After tapping the ball thrice in the same direction he carries the ball to his right side with a reverse stick and then downwards. Before repeating the practice a player should exercise the tapping of the ball to his left side and then to the right side upto a reasonable distance.

The next practice should be done according to the signal of the trainer in order to develop a habit of abrupt change in the direction of the next move.

Speed and control the ball

A player pushes the ball ahead to a distance of about 10 yards, sprints to play again before it becomes dead or is stopped. He dribbles the ball a few steps and then repeats the exercise. The practice can be done on a small portion of the field by going up and down.

A name of ball control

The entire team of eleven players each in possession of a ball, run around rapidly in all directions dribbling and retaining the possession and control of the direction of the ball in a circle of 16 yards radius.

In doing this practice the players should avoid the clash with another player and this can only be achieved without crowding or bunching at one place. Try to move in open places.

The Flick

The flick which in earlier days was very rarely seen, is part and parcel of the modern game. Although as early as 1928, the Indians, in their first Olympic victory in Amsterdam, demonstrated that the flick could be used both as a means of passing and also of shooting at goal, it was more than thirty years before its full significance and possibilities were properly recognised. Even in the middle sixties flicking the ball in mid-field over the head of an opponent to a team mate moving into the open spaces was avoided because of possible danger; it would also have been taken as proof that the player lacked mastery over other techniques. It was only dangerous in those days, because very few players understood how to flick the ball with control and accuracy. Gradually, however, especially among active players, the opinion began to prevail that a ball flicked at goal, and especially a high aerial flick carried out at the correct moment with full regard for the state of the play, demands not only a high degree of technical ability but also a certain degree of mental application. It is just this ability to weight up the right moment to produce a high flick over the head of an opponent, who is marking very tightly, to a fast player on one's own side who is standing unmarked which demands a mental agility that not all players possess.

Indoor hockey and, not least of all, the introduction of the penalty stroke, have contributed to the fact that top class players in the modern game are far superior to those of ten and twenty years ago in the technical execution and tactical application of the flick.

A pre-requisite for learning the flick is complete mastery of the pushed pass.

The basic position, as well as the grip on the stick, is the same in flicking as in pushing. However, as the ball should leave the ground when flicked, the stickhead has to be placed not only behind but also somewhat beneath the ball. That is only possible, however, if the ball is placed a little to the left in front of the left foot and if the upper part of the stick is inclined backwards to the right. As with putting the shot, the weight of the body is then the player emphatically onto the bent right leg, in the side-on position, so that the player can see 'under' the ball.

The action of the flick is initiated by a rapid shift in weight from the right leg onto the left and by the simultaneous movement of the right arm operating along the line along which the ball is being sent. The left arm, on the other hand, presses the stick in the opposite direction and levers the curve of the stick upwards. In the final stage of the flick the ball receives its last impulse from an abrupt movement of the wrist. To produce a hard and accurate flick, the stick and body should follow the path of the ball as far as possible.

Methodical series of drills: from flicking the ball at rest, with the player stationary, to flicking a moving ball when on the run :

1. *Flicking against a wall:* To make the task more difficult, a circle can be drawn, into which the ball has to be flicked, or a line some three or four yards high can be drawn, over which the ball has to be flicked. The distance from the wall is increased in proportion to the increasing mastery of the shot.
2. Flicking with a partner, combined with stopping

the high ball. The distance should be between six and twenty yards.

3. Three players, standing eight to twenty yards from each other along a line, flick the ball to each other. In this practice the ball must always be flicked over the head of the player in the middle to the other outside player. After each flick the player changes with the man in the middle.

4. *'Chase the Ball'*: The aim of this flicking competition, played across the width of a hockey pitch between the centre and twenty five yards line, is to flick the ball over the line at the far end (the side-line of the normal pitch). The game begins with a flick five yards in from one side-line. Where the ball is stopped dead by the opponents, the next flick can be carried out in other direction.

5. *Practice for the penalty stroke:* In order to practise the penalty stroke, the ball is flicked into the left and right hand corners of the goal, along the ground as well as into the top of the goal. Advanced players should also practise disguising the direction of the flick.

6. Flicking the stationary ball while running, the left leg being placed forward at the moment of the flick.

7. Flicking a stationary ball at the goal white running with the right leg being placed forward at the moment of flicking. With this difficult skill, attention must be paid to see that the upper part of the body is inclined well forward and is over the ball.

8. a) After dribbling a short distance the ball should be stopped on the twenty five yard line with the reverse stick and flicked as quickly as possible to another player behind the centre line, who then flicks the ball back over a third player so that this last cannot reach the ball. This should be done successfully ten times.

   b) With increasing sureness in flicking, the ball need no longer be stopped but can be flicked while still rolling.

9. After beating a passive defender ten yards from goal on the right hand side, the ball, still rolling, is then flicked directly at goal without being stopped. The left foot at the moment of flicking should be forward.

10. After beating a passive defender ten yards from goal on the left hand side, the player should flick the still rolling the ball direct at goal without first attempting to stop it. The right foot should be forward at the moment of flicking.

The Half Line

The half backs are three in number. One of them operates in the centre of the ground, the other two on either side while collectively they cover all the ground between the side-lines. They are the hardest worked members of the team. The strength of a team depends on the half back line.

Modern half back play is a delicate and scientific business. Hockey today is a very different game from that played thirty years ago. The rough and ready methods of earlier days are seldom seen. Modern first class halves make more use of the push stroke for passing than the ordinary hit. It is the duty of the halves to get their forwards moving by judicious passes. Too often a half back is content to tackle and rob an opponent and then hit the ball widely up the field in the hope that somehow his forwards will get it. I et halves not forget they are too coordinate the activities of the defence and the attack.

Hockey in the champion country of India is now on the decline chiefly because of the destructive outlook of defence players. Defenders are prone to believe that they have had a successful game it they have prevented any goals being scored against their side. This is wrong. The primary object of the game of hockey is to score goals and the aim of the defence, particularly the half line should be to half the attack with constructive hockey. They do no satisfy the needs of the team by merely destroying the opposing side's moves.

In attack they will be immediately behind their own forwards, closely backing them up, and giving passes to them without delay. Quickness is the essence of their play and it is fatal for them to delay with the ball.

In defence they must relinquish their position immediately behind their own forwards and as quickly as possible get between their own backs and the opposing forwards. Their chief defensive duties are tackling, worrying the opposing forwards and intercepting passes.

Central half. No single player has so much to do with the strength or weakness of a team as the centre half. He is the most important member of the defence and also of the attack. He needs to be a player of more than ordinary skill. It is said that a centre half must be a player of more than average brains. He and centre forward are the schemers-in-chief of the team. They should work in complete unison. No single player has so many duties to perform. He must be here there and everywhere, busy with a thousand odd tasks and making good shortcoming of others. No breathing space is ever his. He is the mainspring of the attack and the sheet-anchor in defence. So he needs to be a player of uncommon energy, versatility, and resources. A quality he should specially cultivate is watchfulness. Watchfulness brings a rich reward. It enables a player to anticipate his opponent's intentions and the direction of the ball.

In defence the centre half's special charge is the opposing centre forward. He must try to shadow him and hamper him at every turn. The centre half needs to concentrate more on the opposing centre forward. Although the backs are mainly and finally responsible for the inner men, when an attack draws near his circle the centre half needs to concentrate more on the opposing centre forward. Sometimes he has to tackle the inside left, and he may do so by means of lightning left hand lunge or right hand thurst. If on the other hand it is the inside right, he has the right hand cut and left hand thurst. Few hard-and-fast rules can be laid down at hockey as it depends so much on circumstances

In attack the centre half must transfer his attention to his own centre forward and his energies to supplying that player and the two inside forwards with plenty of passes. He will find it easiest to pass to his inside left, but it is not the thing that is easiest that the centre half must do, but the thing that is best. He must cultivate the push stroke. It is a matter of judgement which forward he shall pass to. He must make his decision in a flash so that the best situated attacker may receive the ball and act at once. Another important point is the pace of the pass. A common fault of many halves is to take the ball down the field. This gives the opposing halves and backs time to cover each player. As a rule the centre half should pass the moment he sees an opening. He may dribble but he must be careful not to over exercise this ability.

A perfect understanding must exist between the centre half and the halves on either side of him. A lack of understanding may cause, confusion and muddle. At the opening or half-way bully the centre half should stand behind his centre forward and slightly to the left of him, and anything from one to five yards away.

Left half. Good left halves are rare. The position is one of many difficulties and comparatively few attractions. Players prefer something easier and more showy and so there is less competition for this position. The position is essentially one for which the player must specialize. He must work at it, and must work hard. If it is once mastered the position becomes very easy.

The main difficulty of the left half is that the greater part of the game is played on his right side but much of his work is necessary on his left. He is so placed that most of his defensive intercepting must be made on his left hand side and it is difficult for him to tackle a speedy right wing forward.

It is a common tendency with the left half to drift away from the side-line. By so doing he increases his difficulties, leaves the wing forward unmarked and throws his own defence out of gear.

In defence the left half's first duty is to mark the opposing outside right. He is absolutely responsible for that player. To a lesser degree he is also responsible for the opposing inside right. One of his great difficulties is to intercept the passes from inside right to his wing. Here his position in defence is just opposite outside right. In intercepting passes from inside right he can do one of two things. Either he can dash in when he sees the pass coming or else he can place himself between the outside right and his inside player-and it must not be more than a yard or two away from the former. In this case the inside right may try to draw him entirely away from his post, and second outside right may run ahead for a long pass in front of him. If he stands on the side-line, the outside right has little margin to outwit him.

In attack the left half's chief duty is to feed his outside left and inside left. He should not hit hard. The ball must go to the receiver's right hand. Do not lift or sky the ball. To do so makes a bad pass. Another nice device for the left half is to draw the opposing right half. Then the outside left will remain unmarked. He should pass the ball to him with a turn of the wrist only, but without any turn of the body so as not to show his intention. When the game is near the opponent's circle, the left half should hit into it.

Right half. The position of the right half is one of the easiest on the field. The right half's play is similar to that of the left half, the major difference being that they are on opposite side, of the ground. The right half must not operate so near the side-line as the left half. If he avoids this the game will be less on his left and more to his right. He must not drift towards the centre. It should be remembered that if the opposing outside left plays very near the side-line and inside left plays rather wide of him, the right half should change position according to circumstances. Every effort must be made by the right half to prevent dangerous centres from the out side left. If the outside left has run down nearly to the goal line, the right half may taken up a position on the edge of the circle for the diagonal pass that may come.

In attack the chief concern of the right half is the out-side right. The right half should not permit his play to becomes stereotyped. Let him look before he passes. He should refrain from passing to his outside right if the latter is marked. He should use the puss-pass from left to right but when near the circle he may hit or make a push-pass into the centre rather than out.

A centre half in a team plays a role of a co-ordinator and is an originator for both offensive and defensive moves-in other words he has a great responsibility to discharge towards other players. His basic knowledge should be positional play and anticipation of the moves, to keep his position up and down in the centre for maintaining the required covering and assist both forwards and the defence depending upon whether attacking or defending.

His ability to guage the pattern of play in the early stages will help him to plan his strategy to swing the ball right or left and thus taking full advantage of the weak links in the opposition. The use of the wing halves like his two arms will ensure functioning of the half line as one unit.

Full support should be afforded to the forward line and feed the ball to be collected on the run followed by being on their heels in order to sustain the pressure on the attack. Wings must be utilised to the maximum as opening out of the game will play dividends. On the other hand, crowding in the inner three forwards will reduce the chance of scoring.

To achieve the aim of scoring it is essential that the ball is swung in both the directions, leading to dislodging the opposing defence, and it is the prime duty of a good centre half to achieve this object. He has to be alert and very sensitive to the trend of the game, far from a defensive position, an offensive situation can be created which can lead to the all important reward-a goal.

To play a good game as centre half, a player should have :

(a) 100% physical fitness and stamina;

(b) Perfect stopping both while stationary and on the run;

(c) Accurate pushing and hitting

(d) Ball control

All those players having attained an above-average standard are gifted some way in this game and it is one's own determination to develop it by sheer hard labour to achieve the above points to perfection.

Constant and regularly running practice is most

essential to maintain the physical fitness. Intensive training is lacking in the present day players and this is the essential part to attain the topmost position.

Hitting, pushing and stopping practice should be a regular habit with the pivot, for perfection in these will lead to an ideal centre half back play.

Whenever a player is unable to get on to the field for practice,—tapping against the wall both right and left is recommended, for this exercise will develop an eye for the ball.

Forward Line

No doubt every member of the team, should consider himself to be the most important member of the side, but in my opinion the forward line has a vital part to play. The best work of the defence can go waste if the forwards are not capable of scoring goals, not because they don't possess stick work and skill in flicking, pushing and driving hard but due to a lack of the knowledge of correct positioning and a sense of the right time and right place to part with the ball. Generally, forwards show a tendency to depend on their individual efforts. Experience shows that many good centres by wings are brought to nought for want of another forward to find contact with them. It is easy to get a goal if for instance, the inside left is following the play and is at the right spot to meet the right wing's centre.

To fulfill his mission of getting goals the forward should use his skill of dribbling only when he does not find an opening. We would emphasise that be try to create the opening with the help of the nearest half instead of by dribbling. It is important that he must not be lazy and be always ready to go for the ball. Wild centering and inaccurate passing, which are usually gifts for the opposing team, can be avoided if the forward does not indulge in pretty stick work unnecessarily, and get himself into awkward situations. Never try to play to the gallery at the cost of the side. A bad habit prevailing among the forwards these days to take the law in their hands by punishing with the hand or interfering with the stick of an opponent who is obstructing with his body or stick in order to impede the progress of the attack. The best thing for the forward to at such moments is to go on with the attack—and rely on the umpire to pull up the offending player.

Finally, shoot with a short swing if time and space do not permit of a full-blooded hit as you enter the striking circle. It is wrong to dribble inside the circle in order to get yourself into a favourable position to score.

Wing forwards

Wing forwards are often starved of the ball and therefore, develop a tendency to leave the side-line in search of pass. It is a blunder for a wing forward to leave the side-line as he can only be tackled from one side, and has, therefore, only one side to defend. Another error is when a wing forward crosses his opponent's 25 yards line without centering. He is wasting time and allowing the opposing defence ample opportunity for thoroughly marking the three inside forwards.

Left wing. This is the most difficult forward position on the field. A player must possess the pick of the best qualifications of all the other forwards. It is no use thinking of selecting a player for outside left unless he is gifted with exceptional place, and even then there are numerous other points to study before he can hope to become proficient.

The greatest difficulty the outside left has to contend with is the necessity of having to hit from left to right every time. This is doubly increased by the fact that it must invariably be done while running at top speed, and it is here that the average player fails lamentably.

Sometimes the outside left runs with the ball in perfect style, but as he approaches the 25 yards line his troubles begin. The only really correct method to centre the ball is by means of a half right turn of the body. The position of the feet and legs in no way altered, but only the upper position of the body. The stroke is made entirely by the arms and wrists.

Many players foster the idea that they should always centre at the 25 yards line. It is correct if the opportunity is there to do so, but now much bangs on the little word". He must, therefore, use his discretion whether to continue almost to goal-line or even make a dash for the circle and get in a shot himself.

In centering, the ball should be allowed to drop slightly behind the player, but care must be taken that the player is not obstructed.

Another method of centering is by suddenly stopping and drawing the ball back, but it should not be used too frequently as the half back will be on the lookout for it. The reverse stroke is one with which every outside left should be expert. Occasions do arise when the stroke is absolutely essential.

The outside left should always keep between the seven yards line and the side-line until nearing the circle, when he should gradually edge in. By this means he is often able to re-pass the ball to the one of his better placed players.

If a half back is told off especially to watch the out-side left, then how is he to outwit him? Let the outside left continually dodge backward and forward, inside and then out again a few yards, and so on, and all the time be prepared to dash in towards the centre to meet a pass and not to wait for it to come. Few players realize what a vast amount can be gained by such methods as these.

A favourite pass to an outside left is the long diagonal one from the centre forward or inside left between the half and back. He must rely on his pace to reach it first.

In the push-in the outside left is again at a disadvantage with the opposing forward or half back. It is almost impossible to lay down any hard-and-fast rule, as it depends entirely on the position of the various players, and the out side left must use his wits to discover his most profitable plan.

Finally, an outside left should not wait for the ball to come to him, but drop back to tackle and help his halves by worrying the opposing forward and making him pass. By doing this, a wing forward can make openings for himself. Suppose he takes the ball from the opposing outside right, he draws the half on to himself and passes to his inside man who should immediately slip it forward towards the line and let the outside left make a dash for it. If the wing forward does this he will always have an advantage over the half, as her latter has to turn round and get going, while the forward has been nearly full speed all the time and is already in his stride.

The following are, therefore, the main points which make the outside left a successful player:-pace, strategy, brain work, strong and supple wrists, and pluck.

Right wing. The position is easy because any one with average pace and a good eye can play there with moderate success. He has opponents only on the one side of him. His work, therefore, is a whole simple and straight-forward. He can be a great player, if he is gifted with speed, is dashing, has a true eye and has perfect control over the ball.

Apart from certain amount of tackling back and charging out at corners, the outside right is almost entirely an attacking player. He must learn to get back up the field for the clearing hits of his backs, who, when defending their circle, invariably hit towards the side-line. The same is true when the opposing backs hit.

The outside right's normal position is close to the side-line. The purpose is that he may keep the opposing half on his left and get a clear run down. By keeping near the side-line he also increases the half's difficulties by giving him more ground to cover and drawing him away from inside right. He must learn another device, i.e. to push the ball to the left of his opponent, and then to run round him on the other side and gather the ball. During this time he has to run about 5 yards from the side-line. In attempting this trick many outside rights hit the ball either, too straight or too diagonally. It goes either out of play or is stopped by the opposing players.

The outside right must avoid overdoing any single device. Opponents will anticipate it. He must vary his tactics, although his scope is somewhat limited. If the outside right is obliges to run down nearly to the goal line or corner flag, he must centre back to the edge of the circle or right across the mouth of the goal just out of the goal-keeper's reach. If he feels that he cannot pierce the defence, he should pass back to his right half.

The outside right is the player who takes corner-hits on the right side. In the event of a corner-hit from the left side his position is a few yards back from the edge of the circle, so that he can field and bring the ball back if the other forwards miss it. The outside right must keep a careful watch over himself in the matter of off-side.

When passing to his partner he must generally pass in front him, so that the other may take the ball at speed. There is one most important point that the outside right must consider: no matter how good his right half is, he must co-operate with him. He must be very wide awake and constantly on the move, dodging this way and that.

Inside forwards

Crowding is a fault which is probably due to excess of zeal. It must be avoided. The more room the inside forwards can give to the centre forward, the better the latter will be able to manoeuvre for position. Again, if the inside forwards keep away from their centre they will be in better position to combine with their wings, who are too often starved.

Many magnificent passing movements often peter out in the circle because many forwards think they can only shoot if they have time and room for a full-swing. No defending back, if he is a good player, will allow this. Therefore would-be scores, must learn to hit the ball without unnecessarily raising the stick. A short, sharp tap will often make a shot difficult to save, as this gives the goal-keeper no chance to save. When there is no room for a full hit, it is better to flick the ball.

Inside left. Ordinary players find the inside left position very awkward, as the ball is generally on the player's left and to pass it to the centre when going at full speed is a matter of much difficulty. There are two ways of doing this; one by flicking the ball in with the point of the stick reversed, and the other by a half body turn from left to right and a wrist stroke like an off-drive in cricket, or the push-stroke. The former is not safe as it requires a very clever move to make the reverse stroke with any degree of certainty. An ordinary player would miss the ball in nine cases out of ten. To the average player it is not a stroke to be used, except in exceptional circumstances.

The alternative method of passing the ball to the centre is the half-turn of the body and the hit or push-stroke by means of the wrists, which requires much practice.

The correct position for the inside forward is about twelve yards from the side-line, through at times it is necessary to come out a few yards nearer the wing forward. His duty is to keep the outside left well supplied with the ball. With the right half in a natural position for tackling, it is very hard to pass the ball to the outside without first drawing the half back. Two methods are open to the player: the square-pass and the forward-pass behind the half's back. The square-pass is rarely used now-a-days.

Another alternative method is to draw slightly towards the centre and then pass the ball behind the half towards the side-line, so that the outside can reach it before it goes out. Care must be taken when passing to see that the player to whom the pass is made is not off-side. This frequently happens when the one back game is played.

One of the secrets of success at inside left is for the player to have a have a through understanding with his wing partner. The chief fault of the ordinary club forward, especially an inside left, is invariably to delay his pass until he is nearly up to the half back or back. At the push-in the left side forwards are at a great disadvantage, as the opposing players are in a natural position to stop the ball. The best plan is for the outside left to keep well up the field, thereby drawing the half back from the inside left. A very good scheme to try now and again is for the inside left suddenly to dash round the back of the player marking him just as the ball is about to leave from push-in and with reversed stick, the inside left can often outwit the other side. The idea of the stick begin reversed is to enable him at once to get the ball on his right side.

Inside right. It is no more difficult for the side right to feed the outside right, as it is for the inside left to feed the centre forward. The feeding of his partner on the wing is the important job. So many right wing players are starved through the inability of the inside right to supply them with the ball.

The inside right must study two points in particular concerning this position. As outside right is probably not so closely marked as an outside left. The half back is necessarily inclined to come towards the inside player and the inside right can then slip the ball out to his wing. The inside right must always remember that the outside right is usually the fastest forward of the five, and so if he is left unmarked for a moment it is the inside's duty to do his best to profit thereby. If the inside right has approached near the circle he should pass to the centre. If the opportunity presents itself, it is sometimes profitable to give a diagonal pass forward to the outside man, between the half and the back, and trust to the speed of the wing partner to outspace the defence either re-pass the ball to the circle or get in a shot.

The inside right must always be ready to pick up a pass from the outside player if the latter has got away, and if he can dash into the circle and get a shot in, well and good, but in the majority of cases he does more good for his side with a left pass to centre or inside left, both of whom are in a far better position for shooting purposes. The reason for this is that the nearer the goal line he approaches the more acute the goal scoring angle becomes.

From the push-in it in often good policy for the inside right to arrange with his half back some means of giving him the sign that the wants the ball push to him instead of straight along the line towards his opponent's goal. Many inside rights often make a sudden dash inside the five yards area as soon as the ball and are off down the wing before the other players have recovered their positions. It this occurs the outside players should immediately return to his original position. There must be a clear understanding between players, which leads to good combination. It must be noted that an inside right should always follow his own or his partner's shot in the hope of regaining possession should the goal-keeper save it. Another qualification very necessary for an inside is pluck, as he has to charge down the hits of the opposing backs, and in doing so he must not hesitate a moment. One of the drawbacks the inside right has to face is that he is so often tackled on the wing side.

Centre forward. There is no doubt that the centre forward is the most important player in the forward line. He must have qualifications of a high order. He must be a fast and clever dribbler and a good shooter. He is the connecting link between the two wings. Thus, it is rightly said that the ideal centre forward is an opportunist and creates opportunities for others. His duty is to draw the defence upon himself and then to pass the ball to his wings.

The centre half always shadows the centre forward. The centre forward, therefore, must use various methods to outwit him. He should keep the centre half continually on the move any running backwards and forwards and dodging him right the left so that the centre half may not know where the likely to be next.

When nearing the circle the centre forward must be ready to dash in to pick up a pass. If he has a clear opening he should not waste a moment, but shoot at once. When covered, a quick pass to one of the other forwards may be far more profitable. Now-a-days the short passing game is generally adopted, with an occasional long pass to the wings. It is always profitable to feed a particularly outstanding forward or a flank which has overpowered the opposing defence. It is advisable to pass the ball to one of the nearer halves rather than pass to a marked forward.

The centre forward should always be alert and never fail to take all opportunities offered by his colleagues. He should vary his tactics according to the situation, although the best method is to play with his inside forwards in "W" formation.

Credit for a goal goes not only to the scorer but also to the player who created the opening, therefore, never be selfish.

Wing forwards

The main functions of wing-forward are to spear-head and attack during offensive moves and to provide the inside forwards and centre-forward with scoring chances by accurate passing and centres. According to the Indian system of play, they are required to operate along the push-in-line to achieve the mission. This forces the opposing defence to cover the maximum width of the field, thus allowing the inside forwards an opportunity to exploit the gaps for penetration during attack.

The left wing is the most difficult position as compared to the right-wing because he has to centre the ball to his right near the opposing 'D' area. To achieve his aim, four alternatives available to him to centre the ball.

(a) To over run the ball, pivot and then centre with left foot forward.

(b) On the run use back hand stroke accurately.

(c) On the run pivot on the right foot and centre.

(d) Use push stroke for passing.

To bring an element of surprise, players are advised to use different strokes for centering the ball. The first method although more reliable in terms of the accuracy, slows down the pace during execution because the ball is ahead of player and the player has to over-run the ball, turn 90% to the right and then centre it on the left foot. The player should master this stroke so as to reduce the time of execution. This should be used when players feel that by slowing down the pace during execution of the stroke, the opponent is not likely to get possession of the ball. The second method is not very accurate unless the players have mastered the stroke. This method; if used judiciously in a patent method of catching opponent defence on the wrong foot thereby helping other forwards to do the damage. It is through back hand stroke pass from me that Udham Singh left-in scored a goal against West Germany at Melbourne Olympics. At Rome Olympics, in the final match between India and Pakistan when India was down by one goal, I got a pass from right-out, dodged used a powerful back hand stroke when Pakistan goalkeeper was caught in kneeling position The ball went 12 inches off the target and missed the goal and a chance to equalise the goal. The third method is a bit difficult and needs perfection to execute a stroke by turning the trunk to the right and centering it on the right foot. The last method is comparatively easy and can be effective when a back pass through push stroke is executed near the goal line to left-in or centre-forward on the top of the circle.

The positional play of left winger viz other forwards and left-half is very important. Left-wing should develop good understanding with left-in and left-half so that he can interchange positions and functions which is a modern trend to meet the opponent defence. During defence role wing forwards should tackle opponent wing forward and prevent him from making good moves with his team mates.

In todays concept, wing forwards must have the following requisite qualifications:

(a) Possess good speed, stamina and centering skill

(b) Good understanding with inners, half-backs and linkman

(c) Should be versatile, capable of playing as inner, half-back and linkman

(d) Should have a good finish in 'D'.

For all those who are aspirant to become good wing forwards and wish to represent the country, we have the following adorn to give:

(a) To achieve perfection, dedicated effort is required to practice basic strokes.

(b) Discuss your game with inners, left-back and linkman to develop better understanding.

(c) Attempt to maximise your achievements with minimum effort. This is possible if you analytically analyse your strokes and attempt to eliminate redundant movements.

Lastly, there is no short cut to glory except solid hard work.

4

TECHNIQUE OF STROKES

It is not possible to achieve the true enjoyment of the game until players, who are generally keen to pay full scale matches straight way, acquire a knowledge of the technique of its chief strokes. It is a good plan to make the beginners understand that they must first learn how to use their sticks to make the ball travel freely before they are put into play a game.

There is no hard-and-fast rule laid down for the position of the head, feet and hands while playing the different strokes, although footwork plays an important part in making a stroke comfortably. A player, first of all, must know the correct way of gripping the stick. The other principles of the strokes are acquired automatically, by having regular practise individually or in small groups. To achieve success it is essential that all exercises are done in slow motion until a correct technique is acquired. Increase the speed gradually.

The grip

It is essential to know that a player is only considered when he is holding his own stick in his hand and as such the stick needs to be a part of the body all the time and always ready for use, whether the player has the ball or not.

As a principle the left grips the stick at the top with the right hand below to the distance demands for the execution of the different strokes as mentioned in each case.

The chief strokes

Before we mention something about the chief strokes I feel the following method is useful for getting beginners into the correct position to get hold of the stick and enable them to travel the ball with the flat side as well as with the reverse stroke.

Push. The push stroke a executed with the wrists, keeping the left hand at the top of the handle, the right hand about halfway down and the arm and shoulder right behind it. The ball is literally pushed along the ground. The stroke is used for short and accurate passes and is of great constructive value.

Flick. The flick is made with loose wrists, the hands placed together. While flicking the stick is placed just behind the ball. The stroke is executed without making a back swing. It is usually executed while the ball is moving and used for a quicker clearance than a hit. The reverse flick is made with the reverse stick with the object to bringing the ball to the right side. It is a very clever way of outwitting an opponent and when sufficient skill is acquired very attractive to watch.

There was a time when the scoop was used often by the Indians against the continental teams and they had no answer to it. But in the test match, recently played at New Delhi. It was experienced that the West Germany players often gained the ground more to their best advantage by using the perfect flick stroke over the heads of Indian players. Surprisingly the ball was sent hard for thirty yards by this method the some players even sent it much farther and it made difficult for our defence to turn quickly and recover.

To get greater power to the flick the grip should be split that is let the right hand drop down the stick a little way. It is the only departure from the principle of executing the flick stroke meant for shorter distance. It is advisable for our players to master this skill which is the right answer to manoeuvre the man to man strategy.

It is a beautiful and most useful stroke but needs strong wrist and much practice. The following practices are suggested to give strength to the wrists:

1. Grasp the stick at the end with the left hand and the right hand close to it, reverse the stick and push the ball to the right. At the beginning of the stroke, the weight of the body travels forward to the left foot, the right shoulder swing round and the wrists provide the flick. Travel the ball only with the reverse stroke in the direction of making a big circle.
2. Travel the ball in the same way but by grasping the stick only with left hand at the same position.

These two much needed practices, particularly to the Indian players who are very much lacking in using the left flick or push, will give necessary strength to the left hand. The stroke has the great advantage of speed of delivery the ball and is, therefore, useful for a quick clearance. A player not only disguise the direction of his pass but also gives a reasonably strength for left hand tackling.

Scoop. The stroke is made deliberately to left the ball. The stick is held almost flat, just behind the ball with hands apart. It is an illegal stroke if at the time of making it or the dropping of the ball it is dangerous in itself or likely to lead to dangerous play. It should be used very sparingly but it is a most useful trick for a left wing to outwit an opponent by lifting the ball over his stick. It is also effective on heavy and muddy grounds.

Drive. It is a wrong notion that to hit a ball hard it is necessary to swing the stick higher than the shoulder at either end. In fact, a short back swing can send the ball to its destination faster. The speed and forced of the hit depend on footwork, timing and the strength imparted by the wrists at the moment of impact with the ball. Avoid slicing or undercutting the ball as these strokes are illegal.

Lunge. The stroke is made with the stick in one hand, the arm extending fully and body lunging forward on one leg, the knee being bent. This stroke is used to push the ball clear of an opponent's stick when he is too far ahead to be tackled. It can also be employed usefully by forwards to prevent the ball going out of the field either over the side-line or goal-line by lunging at the ball and using that extra reach.

Jab. This again is a one-handed stroke performed with right or left hand, is a poke or thrust at the ball. It is a quick forward jabbing movement of the stick held in one hand with the arm fully extended. It is used for getting the ball before an opponent when two players are reaching for it, one jabs it out of an opponent's reach.

To practice jab and lunge

1. a) Develop ability of a sharp jab at the ball, while holding a stick in one hand with the arm fully extended.

   b) Develop a strong left wrist by playing the ball with reverse stroke while holding a stick in left hand only with the arm fully extended.

2. Two players facing each other keeping the ball in between them at equal distance. A quick sprint to play the ball. Both players should try to play earlier than the other with right hand jab and then with the left hand Lunge.

Constant and relentless practice of these two one-handed strokes is essential. Jab and lunge are to be used only when two handed strokes are impossible. In other words I may say that when a player need a greater reach to play the ball such strokes are very useful.

Dribble. The art of dribbling is most important and a player is not perfect until he has mastered it. But dribbling should be avoided if a push or a hit to another team-mate will serve the same purpose. Players should not attempt to dribble on uneven, bumpy or muddy grounds. The chief object of the dribble is to run as fast as possible with the ball under control, tapping it first to the left and then to the right. The position of the left hand is at its usual place at the top of the stick and the right hand three or four inches below with the ball about a yard in front of the body. Dribble with the stick close to the ball.

Fielding the ball. Experience indicates that the method of stopping the ball with the stick is the easiest and quickest. That is why hands are seldom used. The use of the hand is, of course, essential to get the desired result at the time of receiving penalty corner pushes or when the ball is in the air and above your waist. If the ball is caught with the hand, it must be dropped immediately.

When stopping the ball with the stick the left hand is close to the top of the stick, the right hand halfway down in a loose grip. The hands should give slightly at the moment of impact to prevent the ball from bounding away. A vertical stick ensures a perfect stop. When an opposing forward is rushing after the ball the best and safest method to stop it is to place your stick and body in the line of the ball. If you have the time and space try to stop the ball to the right of the body-an easy position to play another stroke.

Fielding and hitting practice

A and B stand facing each other at a distance of say 20 yards, the centre line marking the middle. A takes a hit to B who stops it and returns it to A, the object being to score a "goal" against each other. A "goal" is scored when the ball crosses the goal-line behind the opponent. To achieve his aim the player has to field the ball properly and hit it back at once. If a feeble hit comes to him he advances to gain ground and tries to catch his opponent on the wrong foot by taking a quick hit in the uncovered space within the ten yard area.

(1) If a player hits the ball over the side-line or extra drawn ten yard line parallel to the side-line the opponent takes a hit from the spot where the ball has crossed over. (2) If a player deflects the ball over a line while fielding it is opponent takes a hit from the spot

from where the ball was deflected. The aim of this exercise is to improve the technique of fielding and hitting; if beaten in fielding to recover or readjust his position quickly. So to gain the best advantage from the exercise each player should be on the look-out to gain ground with speed and develop a quick recovery.

Practice in running to field the ball

The practice should be done within the area of 25 yard and in the direction of side-lines instead of goal-lines. Both the players should try to catch each other on the wrong foot by hitting widely on either side of the player but within the specified area. The chief points to learn how to stop the ball coming out of reach with the left and right hand lunge.

Fielding the ball on the run and abrupt change of direction

A,B and C stand in triangular formation on the edge of a circle of 16 yards radius. A pushes the ball to B who runs forward to stop it and diverts it to C who in turn pushes it to A to complete the triangle. In the second exercise C passes to B and B to A and A to C.

The three big points to remember while carrying out these exercise: (1) To run forward to meet the ball. (2) To try to divert the ball to the third man without stopping it. At the most you may touch the ball twice-once for controlling the ball and the second time for passing it on. (3) To run back to your original position on the circle after executing the pass. Any player responsible for sending the ball out of the circle loses a point. The man with the last number of points against his name wins the game.

Accurate shooting, covering and stopping

Six to nine players stand on the edge of a circle of 16

yards radius with three or four balls to hit and a stump dug in the middle. All the balls are in play at the same time and the object of the players is to knock down the stump. They should always be alert and keep shifting their position in order to stop any hit from any direction that misses the stump. Any player responsible for allowing the ball out of the circle, gets the penalty of running round it with the ball under control.

Practice for developing the skill in interception and tackling

Six players on the edge of a circle of 16 yards radius pass a ball to any one of themselves. Three men inside the circle try to intercept the ball. Any of the three intercepting it changes position with the man who touched the ball last outside the circle. The game can also be played with four men outside and two inside.

Another form of the exercise is to allow the six players to move and dribble and pass anywhere in the circle, with the other three concentrating on tackling and interception.

Similarly, the game can be played with five players-two versus two with one neutral who constantly joins the side in possession of the ball.

Exercise for goalkeeper

Six or seven shooter outside the circle hit the ball to the goalkeeper who covers a stump in the middle. The goalkeeper is supposed to keep turning about and stopping all shots aimed at him, kicking with either foot and quickly clearing to the sides. Every one on the circle should be ready to rush at rebounds from the goalkeeper's pads and to stop or field any shots missing the goalkeeper. All shots and clearances should be made rapidly. As if an actual match. If done fast enough the exercise will tire the goalkeeper in less than ten minutes. To eliminate any waste of time one of the shooters keeps a spare ball ready and the moment the ball in play goes out he calls out to the goalkeeper and continues with the game. Any shooter failing to rush at the rebound or field the ball gets the penalty of running round the circle once with the ball under control.

Ball control and abrupt change of direction

Ten to fifteen players, at least half a dozen of them with balls, move on the double at the coach's whistle. Those without the ball may overtake the others in order to keep their distance. At the second blast of the whistle everyone stops. Those in possession of the balls hit them across the circle to the players who were without one. The exercise is then restarted-first clockwise and then anti-clockwise.

An extension of the exercise would be for the players to turn about and continue without any stop at the sound of the whistle. The object of the exercise is to practise making an abrupt change in direction while on the run.

Dribbling and shooting at goal

Six bottles are placed one behind the other three yards apart upto the top of the striking circle. The player weaves his way with the ball through the bottles. As soon as he enters into the 'D' he shoots at goals.

1. Four teams line up with the ball having four players in each team. All the leading players will move with the ball, keeping it in control, take shot at the goal. On return will pass on the ball to his

second player with hit or push. All the four players complete this practice. The team whose ball will reach first at the starting point after completing the practice will be the winner.

2. The first four players after sending the ball to their second player stand at their positions shown in the diagram. The players of the second line of all the four teams weave their way though the standing players before taking shot at the goal. After sending the ball to their third players, they stand on the positions of 5 to 8.

   The third and fourth players will carry the practice on their turn and release the standing players by taking the positions of their own players. The game completes when players of first and second line weave the players and take shot at the goal. The winner will be determined whose ball reaches first at the starting point.

3. A game can arranged between the two teams consisting of eight or nine players aside. Both teams alternately take up the positions in defence (standing only) as shown in the diagram No. 7 and in attack for the equal specified period. The team scoring more goals will be the winner.

Dribbling relays

(a) Three teams of five men each stand in rows. At the coach's whistle the leaders run to the side-line pick up their balls and zigzag their way between their men standing four yards apart. On their return they weave their way in such a way as to form the figure eight. On reaching the side-line they pass the ball on to the next man who repeats the exercise.

On completing the exercise each player takes his position at the end of his row which automatically keeps moving up to the starting point. The game is complete when all five have performed the exercise. The team to complete it first wins.

(b) Three or more teams consisting of five players each line up inside their fixed areas on a circle of sixteen yards radius. At the whistle No. 1 of each team rushes towards the nearest ball and hits or pushes the ball to No. 2 who after taking it in his stride dashes with it round the circle clockwise. When he is back with his team the returns the ball to No. 1. This is repeated till all the players have gone round the circle. After sending the ball to No. 5, No. 1 will change position with No. 2 and repeat the exercise. The team which completes the whole game and places the ball in its original position first is the winner.

One important rule to remember is that No. 1, or the leader, will not move out of the little circle. If he has gone out to receive the ball he must return to his position inside the inner circle before passing it to the next man. The passes from the leader must also be received in the fixed area meant for the purpose on the outer circle.

Solo practice

(a) Dribble with left hand only to develop a strong left wrist.

(b) Play with two sticks, one in the right hand and the other in the left hand and run pushing the ball with each stick alternately.

(c) Pass stump with reverse flick or push to develop the ability to bring the ball on the non-stick side of an opponent.

(d) Dribble at varying speeds pushing the ball from right to left and left to right along a lane one to three yards wide.

(e) Tap a tennis ball against a wall on your right to practise the reverse-stick stroke.

Practices in hitting and fielding

A game of stopping and hitting the ball to one another (i) between two players (ii) Two-a-side, to be played within 25 yards area while facing the side-line.

Rules

1. Player do not touch or play the ball more than twice when it is stopped on his right side and not more than three times if the ball is received on the left side, before returning to his opponent player or players.
2. If a player hits the ball or deflects it over the lines other than the side line, he losses one point.
3. Player succeeds in sending the ball over the opponent's side line gets one point.
4. The team which collects 10 points first is the winner.

Hitting and stopping inside the circle of 16 yards diameter

Rules

1. Two players passing to each other on the run.
2. The player shall lose the point if he fails to stop the ball inside the circle.

3. Player in his turn after receiving the ball must not return it before he dribbles the ball a few steps.
4. At no time both the players should be in the same half of the circle.
5. Ball must be sent ahead of a player and failing which a point is to be lost.
6. Whosoever score 10 points first is the winner.
7. The game of pushing should also be played in the same way.

Tackling

The game is to be played against each other standing behind the leading player, with the ball at the centre-line having a 2 yards distance between them.

Rules

1. On the signal, the leading player will try to score the goal, keeping the ball closely controlled while running at top speed and the following players is to tackle him from left or right side.
2. The game comes to an end if the leading player succeeds in scoring a goal or the tackler sends back the ball over the centre-line.
3. Second time the reverse game will be played by bringing the tackler as a leading player.
4. Third time the game would only be played to decide the winner if there is no result. The positions of No. 1 and No. 2 should be decided with the spin of the coin.

Points to note

1. Tackler should face towards the centre-line and

leading player should face the goal-line during the tussel of taking possession of the ball from each other.

2. Player is not allowed to touch the body or strike the stick of his opponent before playing the ball.
3. Striking, hooking or in any unfair way impeding the speed of the opponent is not permissible.
4. Tackle should be with held till the ball is little away from the opponent's stick. When the ball is away from the opponent's stick-use *Jab* or *Lungh,* as the situation demands, to get the ball out of a player's reach.

One-a-side and two-a-side games

After completing the bully at the 25 line, the attacking player should try to score a goal and the defending player should defend. Similarly a game of two-a-side is to be played which should be started at centre-line instead of 25 line.

Rules

1. After a goal is scored, or in case of failing to score a goal within two minutes time, the defender will become an attacker and the attacker will defend the goal for the reverse game.
2. The third game will decide the winner in case there is no result in two games. The toss should decide the attacking player for the third game.
3. The player who succeeds in defending more goals or the player who succeeds in scoring goals more than his opponent, in case the game is played for some specified period is the winner.

IX and seven a side competitions

It is strongly recommended to introduce Six-a-side Hockey Tournament in between the players of the same school in order to improve the standard of the game. Such kind of games will assist the players to built up the reasonable stamina required for this fast and strenuous game. Boys will also get the opportunity to play on a different positions instead of one particular position on the field. The modern hockey need such players who should be able to play all the positions except at goal.

The rules of the game of Six-a-side (or Seven-a-side) shall be the rules of the game of hockey except in the following cases:—

Teams and duration of the game

The games shall be played by two teams of not more than six/seven players each. The formation of the team shall be optional. A kicking player used in lieu of a goalkeeper must wear distinctive clothing.

The duration of the game shall be a matter of agreement between the captains or in tournaments by local rule of an organising committee. The duration of the half-time should not exceed two minutes.

Ground. The ground should be of the full size.,

Offside. The rule of two-man offside should be applied instead of Three.

Penalty corner and long corner

Not more than four of the defending team shall remain behind their goal-line. The rest of the defending team shall remain beyond the centre line until the hit has been taken.

Practices-dribbling and shooting at goal

A game of nine players on each side including the goalkeeper to practice dribbling, hitting, stopping and taking shot at goal and at the same time practice to goalkeeper.

1. Each group consisting of four players stand outside the side-lines within the distance of 10 yards from the centre line and the goalkeeper in the goal of their own side.

2. At the starting point only two players will be with the ball to start the game one after the other with the interval of the one minute and the opposite four players will receive the ball on their turn either from the goalkeeper or from the player in practice.

3. The game starts with dribbling upto the circle then shot at goal from inside the circle. After taking shot at goal the ball is to be sent either by the goalkeeper or by the striker himself to the player waiting for the ball on the opposite side, who after receiving the ball will move towards the centre of the field while keeping it in his control from where ball is to be sent by hit or push to his third player. The starting player will take the position at opposite side after sending the ball to his colleague duly taking shot at the goal.

4. The game comes to an end when all the eight players complete the whole practice, that is, they return to their original positions with both the balls.

5. Players should take start and receive the ball only in the area of ten yards from the centre line.

6. No other player should help the receiver in stopping the ball.
7. The winner will be that team whose both the balls reach first at the starting point.

Utilization of maximum number of players on one field

72 players with 8 balls

Practice—Passing, dribbling, tackling, intercepting and developing the skill of finding the gap to give and to receive the ball. Divide the whole field in eight equal parts as shown in the diagram No. 12. Six/five players against three, play the game of intercepting the ball from the players in possession. Detail of the game is given in number 3 diagram.

64 players with 32 balls

Practice—Pushing, Scooping and flicking.

(a) Divide one half of the field into four equal parts by marking a line, joining the centre and goal lines. Five pairs in each part practice various strokes. One pair or two players facing opposite in the direction of centre and the goal line.

(b) In the second half 12 pairs facing centre and goal lines practice hitting and stopping the ball.,

55 players with 11 balls

Practice shooting at goalkeeper.

(a) Seven shooters out side and circle and two goalkeepers (turn by turn). Practice as mentioned in diagram 4.

(b) In the second half, 9 players (six against three) in each part of the field to play the game of interception and tackling. The same game may be played, two against one or four against two, to develop the skill of interchanging positions and to get the pass in the gap.

(c) Practice dribbling and shooting at goal in running.

Five players on each side of the circle towards the side-line move individual with the ball while dribbling and taking shot at goal.

Shooting at the goal

Players No. 3 and 4 are with the ball. The Half-Backs push the ball towards No. 1 and No. 2 Backs. The Backs, after stopping the ball, pass it on the forwards with hits to the far placed players and with pushes to the nearer players. The forwards, after controlling the ball in a proper way, dribble the ball before taking a shot at the goal.

The left-side players carry the ball with control. Before passing the ball to their right they move a little ahead of the ball and with a half turn to the right side, push the ball or hit it. When the ball is coming in speed or to an unfavourable position the shooters should bring the ball within their control before taking the shot. Right side players pass to their left side players who come forwards to take the shot at the goal. Shooters must make it a habit to go for the ball and should not wait or go behind to adjust their hitting positions.

A player on one side of the circle is in possession of three balls. He sends each one of them across to his opposite side players who shoot at the goal. To give a good practice to the goal-keeper the player should take one shot at a time at the goal.

To complete the exercise all the players must change their positions by rotation. A forward is advised to practise shooting at the goal in the following manner:-

From the middle of the 25 yard line-

1. Dribble the ball keeping it close to the stick.
2. Use only two taps in order to move into the circle and shoot at the goal with the third impact.
3. To improve the speed and to cover the distance between the 25 line and the line of the circle in the shortest time, use only one tap before taking a shot at the goal.

Near the side-line—

A player may use one tap more than that given in No. 2 and 3. The wingers should practise this exercise by moving from this place.

Pass the hurdle before shooting

Every player with the ball lines up on the centre line. Dribble the ball in speed before reaching upto the hurdle. To pass the hurdle, a player must use his reverse stick three times to carry the ball towards his right side.

After shooting at the goal, he should recover the ball and dribble back at top speed and with long taps to repeat the exercise.

Three attacking players, each with the ball, line up at the centre line with the aim to score a goal. Six defenders position themselves in defence to block the attackers. They are only allowed to tackle without leaving their places, but they may move either of their feet in order to make their feet in order to make their reach longer.

The attack must go through the defenders before aiming to take a shot at the goal. The return exercise must be done with the change of positions, the defending players score and the attacking players defend. Only the roles are reversed.

Players dribble the ball forward and just before the obstacle dummy with the body and stick feint over the top of the ball towards the left side, then bring the body, stick and ball towards their right to pass the obstacle. They take a shot at the goal as soon as they enter the circle.

Place four to more obstacles on the ground as shown in this diagram. Travel the ball towards the first obstacle and when fairly close, take the ball to your right with a reverse stick and then bring the ball in front again to pass the next obstacle in the same fashion.

Players intending to shoot at the goal must practise to play with reverse stick by placing the obstacle at various angles before taking the shot at the goal.

When more players are available they should assist each other by replacing themselves with the dummy obstacles. They should tackle, but in doing so they must not have their places.

Shooting at the goal on moving ball

Player on both sides are with the ball except the receiver No. 1, who takes a shot at the goal off a pass from another No. 1. The shooter goes behind the goal after taking a shot to pick up the ball till another player relieves him. Passer No. 1, after passing the ball, stays at the top of the circle to take his turn of shooting at the goal. Similarly, the exercise goes on. Players after being relieved from behind the goal should join the second line by taking position at the back of the line to repeat the exercise. Every player should take at least 20 shots at the goal before finishing the exercise.

5

THE HOCKEY STICK

"The equipment of a game adds greatly to one's interest in it. A cricket ball becomes almost a companion and seems in a sense responsible for the runs made off it; and a hockey stick, by reason of its longer life, if kindly treated worms its way even deeper into the affections, and the longer one lives with it the harder it is to discard."

So wrote, a wellknown figure in the Hockey world. But that was in 1895! His subsequent remarks show how the development of the hockey stick influenced the advance of the game.

> "In the days of natural sticks, the pain of parting was even keener, for weapons could not then be turned out to duplicate a pattern to within half an ounces its weight. A whole stock would be inspected to find the nearest shape to one's fancy, and once its little ways were master nothing could dissolve the partnership but decay.

That was in the days of hollies, but earlier, during the first period of the game's revival, it was not so. One has horrible recollections of the time when the man who put up the posts brought a tangled lump of sticks along with him, out of which each chose what suited best.

Those ancient weapons were dumpy affairs in oak, very weighty for their bulk, were brandished in one hand; and applied generously to the ball or shins. It was every man for his own hand then, and the rest followed in his wake and waited till he came to grief. One smiles now at those simple ways, but it is very possible that, were we put back today with such implements into the old fields, we should do no better for all our knowledge of combined warfare. It is the stick-makers and the roller that have made the real improvements in the game, and have left us, if better as a team, individual less expert, and a thousandfold more careful of our shins. We grow graver every year over the dangers of the game, but then one never looked to keep the skin on one's knuckles, and was lucky if none was lost from one's face.

Out of the miscellaneous heap, the property of the club, the evolution of the hockey stick followed natural lines. A binding of string or a planed face gave it individuality and men began to arrive on the ground with their weapons under their arm, to the surprise and some what to the scorn of their club-mates. It seemed to argue superiority thus to distinguish oneself with a special club. But the habit grew, and, as its lavishness began to alter the assessment of sticks from so much a dozen to so much a piece, ash and oak gave way before the rare holly, the face grew wider, and the universal dribbling was occasionally overruled with a big hit.

In fact, the hitting became tremendous; but pernicious as it may have been, it led the way to scientific order. So long as the odds were against hitting the ball at all, if one tried to hit hard, there could be no division of the side into backs and forwards. Each man had to dribble till he lost the ball or his wind, and the nearer his friends kept to him the better their chance of coming to his assistance.

The hollies changed all that; the field began to be spaced out as in Association Football, and the backs had a fine time; for though the hollies were heavy and very seldom ran to the lawful two inches and a half they carried all their weight in the right place and had a spring in their shafts that no "made" stick can approach. Indeed, a practice drive with one on level ground has been measured at 175 yards, a big hit even from a cricket bat, and more than enough to face to close quarters. But the hitter had imported a newer element than danger into the game, and his hitting was applauded, for it soon became, from the difficulties incidental to dribbling with a thin and heavy stick, the salvation of his side.

But the supply of suitable holly was not equal to the demand, and it occurred to an ingenious London manufacturer to replace it with sticks sawn to the required shape out of an ash board. One can recall the interest their appearance caused at a county match, and one remembers, too, how horribly they stung, and how easily they were broken. But since they equalised the struggle between defence and attack, giving the forward another inch of face to dribble with, they gradually supplanted the natural wood, though, when one smashed three sticks in a match, and thirteen in a season, one felt that the outside value had been given for a clean hit.

Method of making stick

Mr. F.G. Howell, the first Hon. Secretary of the Hockey Association (England) 1885-1888, replying to an inquiry from Cape Town, had this to say about the stick then in use and the method of making it.

> "The sticks we use are ordinary maple sticks. We put the ends in boiling water for twenty minutes and then put them under a heavy weight and bend them out. Then when dry and cold, we spoke-shave them down until the face is flat, generally shaving off a alice first. Then we shave the handle down until it is little more than one inch in diameter at the top. The top and face are roughened with a coarse file".

"The hockey stick specified by the Hockey Association in 1887, which had to pass through 2-inch ring and be innocent of any metal fitting or sharp edge, bore much the same relation to many earlier sticks that a rapier bears to a bludgeon. The lighter stick greatly assisted the trend already in progress towards the substitution of speed and skill as the decisive factors in game instead of mere brute force and slogging. It was so much easier to handle that accurate dribbling and passing became possible for the first time, and these entirely new methods required for their exploitation room to manoeuvre and an agreed formation in which each man knew his part and place. By degrees the disposition of players was modified in the direction of fewer places in the forward line and more in defence until the present formation, or something very like it, became standard practise."

6

GENERAL EXERCISES

Two players each with the ball hit simultaneously towards each other. The player after taking a hit, if misses the control of incoming ball losses a point. A practice may be done in a similar manner by using the push stroke.

Hitting, stopping and conditioning

Three players are lined up on each side-line while facing against each other. The first player with the ball takes the hit to his opposite player. The receiving player stops it and moves up a few steps before returning the ball to the second player. Immediately after hitting, the striker sprints across the field in a clockwise direction and takes his turn in the queue.

This practice should be continued till all the players run across the field at least four times. The next exercise may be done with the Push and Scoop instead of hitting.

To utilize more players the second half of the field may be used. Two teams may be arranged to do this practice in a competitive way. The winner will be the team which first complete the exercise.

A game of passing and intercepting

Three players within the circle try to intercept the

passes made between six players standing outside the circle. The successful player changes his position with the player who last played the ball.

Players outside the circle are required to receive the ball and dispose it off only from outside the circle. They should practice giving passes and to receiving them in uncovered spaces. The same exercise should also be practised in a limited area without keeping any restriction on the players in giving pass or in receiving the ball.

Return pass

A player in the middle of the circle pushes the ball to each of the six players in turn. The recipient of the ball stops it and immediately returns it to the player in the middle. Any player who fails to receive the ball inside the circle or allows the ball to go out of it loses a point. The player who loses minimum points wins the game. Every player will have a turn in the middle.

Tackling, passing and anticipation

Three players on one side are ready to tackle six players within the circle. All the six players try to keep possession of the ball among themselves with the skill of dribbling and accurate inter-passing while doing so the players other than the player in possession of the ball must move to an unmarked place and should also be ready to receive the pass given in the open space.

The successful tackler will change his place with the player who last played the ball.

The player responsible for allowing the ball to go out of the circle shall become the tackler in the place of the player who remained as tackler on more occasion than the other two.

Ball out of reach

Three forwards each with the ball and three defenders line up in a straight and diagonal direction respectively. The first forward after pushing the ball well out of his reach runs to take possession of the ball and at the same time the first defender also runs to control it. Similarly, the other two pairs also do the same practice when their turn comes. Instead of allowing the forward to control the ball it is better for the defending player to disturb the ball by sweeping it if it is on his right side and with a reverse stick to the ball on his left side.

This practice is very useful for the defending player who is required to cover his beaten colleague. The forward should use the Jab stroke to avoid the tackling of a defending player and to keep control on the ball away from playing distance.

Retreat and going for the ball

Two groups of four players each line up behind the goal-line. No. 1 and 3 are the players of defence line and No. 2 and 4 are the attackers. At the signal of the trainer the No. 1 players of both the group dribble the ball upto the 25 yards line and return to their starting position leaving the ball at the dotted line. The No. 2 player sprints to bring the ball back. The remaining players No. 3 and 4 of both the groups continue the practice in a similar fashion.

The group whose last player crosses the goal-line with the ball first is the winner.

Covering each other

Two defending player No. 1 and 2 practice controlling the ball pushes in open space. The unbroken line shows the direction of a push and the broken line the direction of the player running to control the ball.

Both players learn the skill of controlling the ball coming from their opposite side. This practice help the players to perfect the tactics of covering the beaten colleague.

To strengthen left hand

In a stationary position, spread the feet about one foot apart and hold the stick with the left hand only. Move the ball and the body in unison from side to side for sometime. Transfer the ball in this manner from one side to the other which assists the player to strengthen his left hand. Move the ball clockwise with reverse stick and towards the direction of anti-clockwise with flat side of the stick.

Repeat the exercise by holding the stick with the right hand.

A six-a-side game

Field 20 × 30 yards, Goal 2 yards wide. Shooting Area one yard from each goal-post.

Rules-No. Off-side

Both the teams consist of six players each and each player in the side has a particular player to mark in the opposing team and only he is permitted to tackle that opponent and vice versa.

Players practice in this game to deliver the ball to each other in open spaces as very player is being marked by his opponent.

A six-a-side should also be played on full ground without any restriction except that the players must deliver the ball before playing it fourth time at stretch.

The rules of the game apply except the following rules:-

1. Off-side: There be at least one opponent nearer to their own goal-line.
2. Corner and penalty corner: Not more than four of the defending team shall remain behind their goal-line.
3. Team may play in any formation but preferably without a goal-keeper.

7

BEATING AN OPPONENT

In a match every player should do his utmost to work for the benefit of his side and to be careful not to do anything which might detract from this. While holding on to the ball unnecessarily (especially attempting to get round an opponent) hinders rather than helps the side's interests, a quick and well-conceived pass to team-mate is usually more profitable. However, on occasions, it is necessary to hold on to the ball to beat an opponent as situations frequently arise, especially for those players who spearhead the attack, in which no team-mate is available for a pass. There are various methods of getting round an opponent. If a player always uses the same one, then the person marking him will soon find the defensive answer. Success in beating opponents depends, therefore, not only on correct technical execution but also on variation. Thus a good player is required not only to know of the various methods of beating an opponent but also to have complete mastery over them.

1. The simplest method of beating an opponent is to push the ball past him on his reverse stick side and then, after a short sprint round to his opponent's left, to take possession of the ball again. Pursuit, after an attempt to tackle has failed, generally costs

the defender so much time that forward is already out of range.

This method of beating an opponent is especially profitable when the pace of the game is hot. But it is important to see that the time elapsing between the ball being pushed forward and being brought back into possession again is kept as short as possible. Pushing the ball past the opponent must take place neither too early nor too late. The choice of the exact moment is generally the deciding factor for the success of the attempt. If at all possible the dribbler should look up form the ball and then push it past the opponent when the latter begins his attempts to tackle.

If the player pushes the ball forward too soon, the defender realises what his real intentions are and will almost certainly halt the attack. But if the forward pushes the ball round the opponent too late, that is to say, within the immediate range of the defender-which happens very frequently-he runs the risk that the ball will hit the defender's stick and be lost.

Methodical series of drills for learning how to beat an opponent by pushing the ball past him.

a) Two groups of players line up opposite each other about seventy yard apart. Between each group six flags are planted at twelve yard intervals. The players pass the ball to the right of each flag and then run round it to the left.

   Having completed the six attempts at rounding the flags, the player passes the ball over to the next player in the other group.

b) A mistake commonly seen in the course of his simple method or rounding an opponent is that the ball is brought too close to the defender. In this case the defender can win the ball without any great difficulty, before any attempt to round him can be made, simply by use of the defender's reach. As an indication, therefore, of a player's reach, a second flag is laid on the ground in front of every upright flag, so that it points towards the player. The dribbler now has to push the ball past the upright flag before reaching at one of the ground. In contrast to a) above this is only practised in one direction.

c) Six players, who form passive opposition, take the place of the six standing flags. However, the flags lying on the ground in front of the defenders indicating their reach, remain.

d) This time the flags on the ground are also removed. The players should now indicate the extent of their reach by lunging forward and going through the motions of tackling, so as to give the dribbler an idea of the exact spot at which the ball has to be pushed past the defender.

e) The players now provide active opposition but are not allowed to retreat in defence. In this practice, the attackers should learn to keep a careful eye not only on the ball but also on the defender. At the precise moment that the defender attempts a tackle, the dribbler must put the ball past him. After this 'stratagem' the dribbler runs round the defender with a short burst of speed and regains possession of the ball behind the defender.

f) The simple method of rounding an opponent by pushing the ball past his left-hand side, or even through his legs, is always used when the defender commits the tactical error of moving in to take the attacking forward.

The forward runs up to the standing defender and stops the ball suddenly on the reverse stick about three yards outside the defender's reach. At this, the latter generally lunges will forward, which the attacker was anticipating and for which he is therefore fully prepared. The moment the defender begins his tackle, the attacker pushes the ball past him or lifts it slightly over his stick.

Playing the ball through the defender's legs is generally not as successful as playing the ball round the defender's body, because the defender can, and frequently does, stop the ball illegally by quickly closing his legs. If however, the player feints before then pushing it through the defender's legs, his chances of success will be much improved. An example: after dribbling on the right the forward takes the ball in front of his body, just before making the attempt to round his opponent. Whilst still outside the reach of the defender, the ball is suddenly pulled about a yard of the left of the player's direct path and then, immediately afterwards, it is passed with the reverse stick, diagonally to the right, through the legs of the defender, which are now wide open. The success of the attacker's deception derives from the ball being pulled sideways to the left which then causes the defender to alter his basic position. This change in stance generally produces a movement to the right, thus forcing the legs further apart than usual. The moment the defender follows the sideways movement of the forward by moving his legs further apart, it is now a simple matter to place a reverse stick pass through his legs.

2. Another method of beating an opponent is to break away suddenly from the straight line along which the forward is running and to begin to dribble the ball in a wide are to the left or right of the defender. Whilst dribbling the forward watches carefully to see whether the defender is following or not. If the defender does not, the forward should dribble straight past the defender with an explosive burst of pace into the open space. If the defender sets off in pursuit of the attacker, however, the latter, after his first, misleading movement, suddenly carries out, quite unexpectedly, a second intentional movement in the opposite direction.

   Only after a certain time lapse can the defender manage to follow this second movement, for which the attacker was fully prepared but not the defender. In fact, by the time the defender has been able to halt his initial movement and follow the forward, who has dodged off in the direction, the forward has generally been able to get completely free to one side or the other. If unexpectedly the defender is not shaken off by this sudden change of direction, the attacker, whilst still out of the defender's reach, has to try dodging back again along the direction of the very first movement.

   A further slight variation for beating an opponent by means of a sudden change of direction is best illustrated by the following situation: the centre forward has broken past the centre half and is now bearing down alone on the opponent's circle. Since he is on the point of entering the circle and getting in a shot at goal, the left back, having rapidly summed up the situation, decides to take the centre forward and so runs across to meet him. A good centre forward will notice this, however, and, just before the back reaches him, will change direction. Keeping outside the back's reach, he dodges to the right, dribbling the ball for a few paces in the direction from which the back has just come, thus causing the back to run past him and allowing himself to dribble on to goal. This method of getting round the opposition, which is not frequently seen, demands considerable practice. But when carried out carefully and with concentration, its success will delight the forward and, above all, will increase his self-confidence.

Drills

a) The player runs in a 'sideways-V' path while dribbling the ball. When he reaches the point as far left (or right) as he wants to go, he suddenly stops on his left (right) foot, and simultaneously plays the ball, without first stopping it, back to the base of the 'V', using reverse stick (forehand).

b) The centre-forward stands with the ball on the twenty-five yards line and the left back, without a ball, off to the forward's right on the edge of the circle. While the centre forward should follow the quickest path to get into the circle, the left back sprints towards him to prevent him from getting in his shot at goal. By means of a sudden change in direction to take him along the line which the back is following to tackle him, the centre forward lets the left back pass by on his left and thus gains time for his shot at goal.

But when the back is slow that he is unable the forward, who has started off on the coach's signal at the same moment, the forward should run straight on and shoot at goal without bothering to try and get round the back first.

Because of the risk of injury when the defender starts from the other side of the circle (the defender in this case trying to prevent the centre forward's shot at goal with a reverse-stick tackle), the forward should only shoot at goal when he has first rounded the back on his left hand side.

c) As a variation of b) above, the right or left back makes a bad clearance and passes straight to the opposing centre forward; after passing the ball, he tries to prevent the centre forward from shooting by sprinting back to the circle.

3. The favourite and the most common way of beating an opponent is to pull the ball suddenly out of his reach to the left or right. Whereas players on the right hand side of the field prefer to go round their opponents on the right, almost all players, whose positions are on the left hand side of the field, prefer to beat their opponents on the left. A few defenders--class players; the man they are marking stands hardly any chance in a duel between the two, unless the player gives up his habit of always trying to beat his opponent on the some side. A forward trying to be as successful as possible at beating a defender, should be equally good

therefore at beating him on either side and, in the match itself, should take care to vary the methods.

Methodical series of drills for beating an opponent to the right:

a) Six yards in front of the player practising stands a flag representing the imaginary defender. During the approach to the flag, the ball is dribbled normally in front of the body to the right. Just before reaching the flag, however, it is brought across the body, midway between the feet, so as to make it easier to play the ball diagonally off the right with the reverse stick.

As the same moment that the ball is pulled quickly to the right the player pushes off powerfully with his left leg towards the right. A powerful movement enable the player to escape the reach of the opponent more quickly.

About three yards away from the flag, the ball is overtaken and dribbled to the right in the direction of the opponent's goal.

b) Two players, each with a ball, stand opposite each other about twelve yards apart. Between them is a flag which they must both beat simultaneously on the right hand side. After beating it, they then run straight to their opposite number's starting position and from here, they begin a new attempt at beating the flag at the same moment that their partner sets off. The simultaneous beating of the flag has a specific purpose; it forces the players to look up from the ball and keep an eye on their partner.

As an indication of the defender's reach, two flags are placed on the ground, in front of the upright flag, in the path of both players. These flags will force the two players to pull the ball to the side at the right moment.

c) Beating an opponent on the right hand side can be made more automatic by playing round flags lined up at twelve yard intervals. The second player begins when the man in front of him has beaten the second flag.

d) When the skill of beating an opponent on the right hand side has been sufficiently practised by means of these three preparatory exercises, passive opposition is then introduced. The player acting as defender is only allowed to lunge forwards (but not to the side). In order to ensure that the defence does in fact remain passive, the defender's right heel must remain in constant contact with the flag behind him. After a few attempts at beating his opponent, the attacker will soon work out that he can always beat the 'anchored' defender when he begins his attempt at the correct moment and remains out of his opponent's reach. At this stage the attacker's attention should be drawn to the necessity for a high approach speed when rounding an opponent.

e) As in c) above but with passive defenders instead of flags.

f) Four defender from a square. Their sphere of action is again limited in that their right heel must always be touching the flag behind them when they lunge forward. The six attackers continue beating the four passive defenders for two minutes, after which the coach changes the defenders and attackers round.

Methodical series of drills for beating an opponent to the left:

a) Six yards in front of the players stands a flag which has to be beaten to the left. On the way to the flag the ball is dribbled to the right of the body; just before reaching the flag, it is brought across the body, midway between the feet, and then suddenly is moved absolutely square to the left. At exactly the same moment that the ball is pulled sharply sideways, the player pushes off powerfully with his right leg towards the left. After two or three paces towards the left the ball is stopped on the reverse stick and dribbled on again in the orthodox manner.

When beating an opponent or flag on the left hand side, special attention must be paid to see that the ball is played left at right angles, i.e. completely square, to the dribbler's normal direction. If this is not heeded and if the ball is played diagonally forwards into the reach of the defender then he will have no difficulty in a match in taking the ball away from the attacker.

b) Between two players practising is flag which must be beaten by both of them simultaneously.

In this it is not always necessary, as in a) above, for the ball to be stopped first with the reverse stick after pulling it sideways to the left. It can also be placed directly onto the right hand side of the body with the reverse stick without having been stopped.

c) Four flags (at twelve yard intervals) must be beaten on the left on after another. Four attempts to beat the flags on the first run are followed by a further four attempts to beat the flags on a return run. This practice can also be carried out in the form of a slalom relay.

d) Getting round the left hand side of one of several defenders indicated by flags, is now followed by attempts to get round the left hand side of a passive defender, whose right heel must not leave the flat behind him as he attempts to tackle. In the course of this practice the attacker must learn not only to look at the ball put also especially at the defender's stick. At the very moment that the defender starts to make his tackle, the attacker must whip the ball square to the left, pick it up with the reverse stick and the immediately place it back again into the normal dribbling position on the right hand side of the body.

e) Beating four passive defenders without pausing.

f) Beating four passive defenders, alternating left and then right or right and then left.

g) Beating four defenders, who once again must remain anchored to the flag behind them. The player practising must beat the first defender on the left hand side but he can choose to beat the second defender either on the left or the right.

4. A particularly promising method of beating opponents for top-class players is to combine beating them on the left with beating them on the right.

   The player begin to beat his man on the left (or right) as described in 3 above. After having pushed the ball far enough to the left (or right) out of his opponent's reach, he suddenly dodges off to the right (or left) immediately after having taken one pace sideways in the same direction as the ball. The ball is then taken to the right (or left) as the player changes to this direction, so that the defender is left wrong-footed and can then be easily passed.

5. Beating defender either on the left or the right hand side, this time introducing a stick dummy. While dribbling, the player suddenly pulls his stick over the top of the ball to one side, without in fact touching it.

   If the opponent is taken in by this deception, the player immediately takes the ball, which has been rolling straight on, to the opposite side. When beating an opponent on the right (left) hand side, the dribbler, immediately before pulling the ball across the reverse stick should feint to move the ball to the left with the stick in the normal position.

   The stick dummy should be practised both when standing still and when running, both when confronting a stationary and a moving opponent.

6. Beating an opponent on the right (left) hand side coupled with a body swerve.

7. Beating the right (left) hand side of opponent by using a stick dummy and simultaneous body swerve.

   When beating an opponent in this way, the player shifts the weight of his body in the same direction, and at the same time, as he dummies with the stick in the same direction. By means of an abrupt push-off from his right (left) leg in the opposite direction, combined with a feinted pass to the left (right), the forward then pulls the ball to the right with the reverse stick or conversely to the left with the forehand in order to break free from his opponent, who, because he has been deceived, can only challenge again after some delay.

Methodical series of drills for learning how to beat an opponent by means of a stick dummy and simultaneous body swerve:

a) The ball is placed eighteen inches in front of the player. The stick dummy and simultaneous body-swerve are carried out first to all with the player stationary in front of a flag. In the first stage, the player passes the stickhead over the ball and moves his body to the same side. In the second stage, he sways in the opposite direction and pulls the ball to the right or left, as the case may be.

b) After a short approach run, the stick dummy and the body-swerve are carried out with a stationary ball in front of a flag.

c) The player runs, without the ball, to a flag six yards away to pick up a ball placed there and attempt to beat the flag in the same way as in a) and b).

d) The player now practises beating a flag while dribbling slowly on the right.

e) The player attempts to beat an opponent who is standing still; after dribbling slowly he tries to combine a stick dummy and a body-swerve. The player must take care to begin his attempt at beating his opponent a good three yards in front of him; otherwise he will come into the defender's reach and run the risk of losing the ball.

8. Beating an opponent on the right (left) hand side,

coupled with a double body-swerve. This method is not so frequently used as the other methods described above, since it is very difficult to carry out correctly.

The player, attempting the dummy, sways first one way and then the other. After the second shift in weight, the upper part of the body returns to its original position and the ball is taken past the opponent in the direction of the original dummy.

Methodical series of drills for learning how to beat an opponent using a double body-swerve:

a) The players carries out the swerve both ways without a ball. His last movement is to dart off in the direction of the original body swerve.

b) The same practice, in front of a flag.

c) The same practice, facing an opponent who merely follows the movements of the practising player.

d) The player practising places the ball in front of himself, performs the two body-swerves whilst stationary and then pulls the ball sideways in the direction of the original swerve. During both body-swerves, the ball must not be touched.

e) As in d) above but this time with a passive defender, who merely follows the movements of the player practising.

f) The exercise is now practised with the double body-swerve whilst dribbling, first of all in front of a flag and then , finally, in front of a defender standing still.

The player, whilst dribbling, has now get past a slowly approaching opponent.

h) Finally the player can choose to beat the defender on either the left or right hand side, using the double body-swerve.

Beating an opponent successfully is an art which not every player can master. It can only be achieved and used successfully in the match after constant practice.

All players must be able to stop the ball safely and cleanly is a pre-requisite for a good game of hockey and a good personal performance depends on it. Stopping is a skill which very few players manager to master completely. It is difficult to hit the ball when running at speed but to absorb its speed and stop it so that it stays at the end of the stick without bouncing off to one side, depends considerably greater skill.

The many small irregularities in a hockey pitch make stopping even more difficult; they almost always compel the player to stop the ball first, rather than pass directly. Uncertainties about stopping leave the wingers and wing halves at a special disadvantage for the ball normally rolls out of play from a bad stop and play has then to be interrupted.

Any unsureness in stopping is not only attributable to mistakes of technique and lack of footwork when trying to get into the correct position, but is also frequently caused by concentrating insufficiently on the approaching ball. Stopping is a test, therefore, of both skill and concentration. It is often to be noticed, especially among young players, that their thoughts, even while they are in process of executing the stop, have already turned to the problem of beating the opponent, having a shot at goal or making the next pass. The result of this 'next step' thinking is that the act of stopping the ball lacks the necessary care and, above all, concentration, so that the ball is not brought under control.

A good hockey player must be able to stop a ball hit from any direction to speeds which vary enormously.

Thus he has to estimate not only the speed of the approaching ball but also have sufficient speed, mobility and skill at his disposal to enable him to get his body and stick quickly into the desired position. The faster the ball, the quicker the player must get the stick behind the approaching ball to bring it under control. For the person receiving the ball, the stopping of inaccurate passes makes particular demands on his speed, mobility and skill, while an accurate pass is relatively easy to stop.

Quite independently of whether the ball is relatively difficult or easy to reach, the player must then attempt to take the approaching ball, even in a difficult situation, so as to be able to use it again quickly without time being wasted teeing it up. The prompt passing on of the ball is only possible, however, if the player receiving the ball has already checked up on the position of his own side and of his opponents before the receives it.

The modern hockey player observes the old tactical instruction 'stop, then look' in reverse. The speed of the game now demands this.

More should be demanded in the final count from very good players; they should be able to feint with movements of the body while stopping the ball, so as to make the opponent run into the empty space. If a feint is carried out before the ball is received, considerable advantages can often be derived, especially for the player about to receive the ball.

The stop can be divided up into various different aspects. According to the position of the player to the ball, we differentiate between stopping to the front and to the side; and according to the height of the approaching ball, between low, medium and high balls. But we could also add as possible divisions: stopping while standing and while running, stopping the ball with the stick and the hand, as well as stopping on the forehand and reverse side.

Stopping on the forehand

There are four possible ways of stopping a low ball:

1. The player faces the ball, as he waits for it with his feet wide apart. During the stop, the stick is held (with the stick face pointing forwards) centrally in front of the body between the two feet which point towards the approaching ball.

2. In this case the player also waits for the ball, facing it and with the legs apart. But the stick, instead of being held in the middle, is now held upright in front of the right foot which is turned sideways. Whilst the left foot is pointing in the direction of the approaching ball, the right foot points to the right following the direction of the toe of the stick.

3. The player waiting for a pass from the right, for instance the outside left, waits for the ball with his feet in a striding position. The feet are at right angles to the line of the approaching ball. If the left foot is advanced, then the stick is held directly in

front of it. The pelvis is parallel to the line of the approaching ball, whilst the trunk is turned to the right through 90 towards the ball, so that the body has to be twisted round in order to receive the ball.

4. The player, with feet apart, waits for the ball coming from the left hand side, so that the left shoulder points towards the approaching ball. The stick is held at a comfortable distance some twenty inches in front of the body and between both feet. During the stop the toe of the stick points in the same direction as the feet.

The four possible ways of stopping on the forehand are all to be seen frequently in the course of the game. Every good player should be acquainted with them and be able to use them appropriately whenever necessary.

During a stop to the front the weight of the body is evenly distributed on both of the legs which are bent. The trunk is somewhat inclined forwards because the right hand is gripping in the middle of the stick or even a little lower. In fact, the lower the right hand is, the easier it is to move the stick quickly to the ball. The stick is gripped from above, so that the back of the hand faces away from the player stopping, who will not be able to see his left thumb. In addition the left hand should incline the stick a little forwards the ball to avoid the possibility of the ball bouncing off the head of the stick.

Much more important, the grip with the right hand should be kept slack, so that the player is always able to bring the face of the stick into the desired direction of the ball which does not always travel straight towards him. Furthermore, while stopping, one must take care to see that the left forearm forms an almost straight line with the stick, and is not bent at the left wrist.

The ball is stopped in front of the body, directly beneath the player's eyes. As the final position of the stop corresponds to the initial position of the stop corresponds to the initial position of the push from the frontal position, the ball can be moved again very quickly after being gathered. Quick hitting of the ball to the front is not possible, however, after a frontal stop. For this, the body must either assume a sideways position to the ball or the player must stop the ball to the side.

Besides necessitating an accurate assessment of the speed and direction of the ball, stopping to the front demands quick, skilful footwork. That alone allows the player to adjust his position in relation to the ball in such a way that it is properly 'in his sights'.

Drills:

1. Two players stand four yards apart, face to face, in the basic position. They play the ball to each other in such a way that the receiver stops it between his feet and pushes it back using the frontal position. The position of the feet must be altered if the ball arrives too far to the left or right.
2. Two players, standing six to eight yards apart, hit the ball deliberately inaccurately to the left or right of the other player. By dint of quick positioning before stopping, the receiver should always stop the ball in the frontal position. Stopping on the reverse stick side should not be brought in with this drill.

3.a) Three players stand a yard apart on the side line of the field; a passer stands in front of them about seven yards away. The passer plays the ball to player no. 1, who, after a stop to the front, passes the ball back. Then the ball is passed back to player no. 2 and so on. When the passer has pushed the ball to the last player in the line, the competition, in which other groups of similar ability take part for purposes of comparison, is completed.

b) Variation: When the passer has played the ball to the last man in the line, he joins the end of the line while the last player with the ball takes over as passer.

The competition is over when each player has had one turn as passer.

c) Variation: instead of a relay practice with the players in line abreast, a relay with the players in single file can also be formed. After each return to the passer, the front man goes to the end of the line. Which group gets its first player back to the head of the line first? Or, if an accurately passed ball is not stopped by the player, he has to fall out of the line. Who is the last player left in?

4. The most difficult drill is a circular relay using two balls. Four players, spaced about four yards apart, from a circle, facing inwards. In the middle of the circle is a passer using two balls. He passes one ball accurately to player no. 1 and, directly afterwards, the second ball to player no. 1 and, directly

afterwards, the second ball to player no. 2. Meanwhile he receives the first ball back from player no. 1 and he immediately passes it to player no. 3. This continues until the last player in the circle has received the ball. Care must be taken to see that this drill starts very slowly but, with increasing sureness, the tempo can be raised.

A competitive element can be introduced by forming a second circle of players.

5. Competition hits: two players face each other at a distance of 22-30 yards, standing in goals of 10-12 yards width. The aim is to score the most goals from free hits.

Stopping that ball to the side is, by comparison with taking the ball to the front, much less certain to succeed. Because the ball is not properly in the receiver's 'sights', but is moving to the side of the body, it is difficult to follow and assess as accurately its direction and speed. A poor stop frequently results from the fact that the ball is not travelling directly along the player's line of sight. On really flat pitches, as for instance on artificial turf or indoors, the ball does not jump. In these cases, the extra footwork required to bring the player into the frontal position is not necessary, so that the side-on stopping, with the stick parallel to the ground, is the most usually favoured method of taking the ball. This, in contrast to frontal stopping, allows a quicker and more powerful pass, either by means of a hit or a pushed pass from the side-on position.

In modern hockey, where forwards are frequently very closely marked by the opposing defenders, the ability to stop to the side, especially by the forwards, becomes much more important. If the ball is passed from behind to an unmarked forward, he should, in order to avoid obstructing when taking the ball, stop the ball, not in a frontal position with his back to the man marking him, but to the side or even with his back towards the passer. In the latter case, which is to be seen relatively rarely, the toes of the forward point in the direction he will take to goal and the head and shoulders are moved towards the side from which the ball is coming, so that he is able to follow it carefully.

At the same time, the stick-face is placed towards the direction from which the ball is coming. If it reaches the forward on the left hand side, it will be stopped on the forehand but facing backwards; if it arrives on the right hand side of the attacker, it is stopped on the reverse stick. With this method of taking the ball, which involves twisting the body round, the ball is not always to be stopped dead. For tactical reasons, it is sometimes better merely to take the pace off the ball-with the player who is making for his opponent's goal adjusting his running speed to the speed of the approaching ball-in such a way that taking the ball can be translated without delay into a dribble at top speed leaving the surprised opponent standing.

To avoid obstructing while taking the ball, the very closely marked forward should be expected, therefore, to be able to stop to the side or, even better, to run to the ball in order to get away from the opponent at the same time collecting the ball to the side: a defender on the other hand should prefer, as far as possible, to use the less risky frontal stop.

All the drills already mentioned for stopping on

the forehead to the front, can also be used, by means of a slight change in position-i.e. moving sideways to the ball-for learning to take the ball to the side. Further drills for practising the stop will be introduced in connection with the reverse stick stop.

The reverse stick stop

Nowadays the reverse stick stop has become just as important as stopping to the right. In earlier days it was avoided as much as possible and players were sometimes even stopped from using it on the grounds of the player's lack of technique and also because of the long blade which made it difficult to turn the stick over quickly. Nowadays, however, the beginner must grasp the reverse stick stop right from the start of his hockey career. A young player's skill and his ability to learn are not the only factors in favour of doing so. If the young players masters the reverse stick stop from the beginning, he will then avoid turning the body unnecessarily when taking the ball; in early practice games this could otherwise lead to frequent obstructions and thereby to injuries as well.

In contrast with the normal stop, the ball is always stopped on the reverse stick in the side-on position. The player can do this in two possible ways:

The Stick is held in the Indian dribbling position, that is: the right hand grips it loosely in the middle whilst the stick is being turned; the left hand grips rather more firmly coming from above onto the handle right at the top. The right shoulder of the player, who stands with feet apart, points towards the approaching ball. So that the ball, when passed from the right, does not hit the back of the stick, the left hand has to turn the stick through 180 anticlockwise, the right hand being left slack. Thus the stick head describes a semicircle above the moving ball. Only if the flat side of the stick is now facing the ball after the turn through 180, with the toe pointing to the ground, can the reverse stick stop succeed. To avoid the ball jumping upwards or bouncing off, the ball should run past the body until level with the left foot, before it is stopped. The reason being that, if the stick is level with the left foot during the stop, the face is slightly inclined towards the right, thus reducing the chances of the ball bouncing off. The player should note the position of his hands on the stick when he has successfully stopped a ball level with his left foot in this way. The back of the right hand should be pointing to the right and the back of the left hand should, at this stage, be pointing downwards.

However as the player can develop only very little power with the left hand gripping underneath the handle in this manner, he is frequently all to easily dispossessed after a reverse stick stop, especially when the left hand alone is holding the stick. To prevent this and to make it possible for the player to produce an effective pass immediately after this stop, it is advisable for him to let the left hand slide round to the right, so that the back of the hand now points to the left. This grip alone will guarantee the transmission of full power from the arm to the stick thus permitting effective reverse stick play.

The position of the player in relation to the ball is the same as in the first example of the reverse stick stop. But this time the right hand alone is turning the stick face. The grip of both hands is kept slack. The fingertips of the right hand turn the stick.

One must distinguish the different movements of the stick face as it goes to meet the ball when using either to the two methods of reverse stick stop. In the first method the face points firstly to the left, then in going over the ball diagonally downwards to the ground, and finally, during the moment of stopping, towards the right; in the second method, the face points firstly to the left, in just the same way, then, however, in going between the feet and the direction of the approaching ball, forwards and finally during the moment of stopping, again to the right.

As this variation of grip during the reverse stick stop allows the stick face to be placed much more quickly behind the ball, it is used especially for stopping the hard hit ball and for taking short distance passes. In the interests of methodical coaching, however, the beginner should initially only be shown the normal reverse stick stop. It can be taught without any great difficulty, once he has mastered the Indian type of dribbling.

Drills for practising the reverse stick stop with the player stationary

1.a) Two players face each other approximately ten yards apart. One of them has a ball. Between them a third player positions himself in such a way that his right shoulder always points in the direction of the player in possession. Whereas the outside players always pass the ball to the player in the middle from the normal position and stop it to the front on the forehand, the player in the middle stops the pass on the reverse stick side and then passes the ball, from the normal position, to his left.

b) The same drill with several three man groups. Which middle player stops the ball on the reverse stick side most frequently within the space of two minutes?

In addition in this drill, the stick face shall only be turned towards the ball when the pass actually been given by the outside player. When this drill is carried out at speed, there is no break between stopping and passing.

c) As in a). After the reverse stick stop, the player in the middle feints to give a reverse stick pass to the right (back to the passer) by pulling the toe of the stick along the ground towards the right but keeping it in front of the ball. The ball now lies between stick and body by means of this piece of stick deception; it is therefore hidden from his opponent and temporarily out of his range. The effect gained by this stick deception is reinforced by a slight shift of weight from the left foot onto the right and, immediately afterwards, the player in the middle sweeps the ball to the left instead with the stick in the normal position.

d) As in a). The middle player ceases to alter his position in relation to each passer. Thus the stops the first ball on the reverse stick side and then gives a normal pass, but the return ball normally to give a reverse stick pass and so on.

e) The same with several groups of three to

form a competition. Which middle player produces the greatest number of reverse stick stops in the space of the two minutes? These are to be counted out aloud by the player himself.

f) As in d). The player in the middle feints to pass the ball, after every stop, to the side from which it has just come.

g) The same arrangement as in d). After the first pass to the player in the centre, the players change places as follows: player no. 1 passes to player no. 2 and immediately runs to take no. 2's place. Player no. 2 stops the ball, plays it on to no. 3 and runs to the position vacated by player no. 1 and so on. Thus, when a player finds himself in the middle, he must always run off in the opposite direction to the ball after giving his pass, whereas the players at each side must run after the ball into the middle.

2. Circles, each made up of six players, are formed. The space between each individual player should be about four yards. Each circle has one ball which one player passes to his left to the next player on the coach's command. When passing with the forehand special attention must be paid that the ball is being passed to the next player about a yard in front of his body onto the reverse stick side. The winning group is the circle in which the ball is returned first to the original passer. The game can be made more exciting if the ball has to go round the circle, two, three or four times.

The following rules must be observed in this competition.

a) Every player must take his turn in passing.

b) If the ball is stopped on the forehand instead of on the reverse stick, the stopper must return the ball to the passer.

c) If a player fails to bring a pass under control with the reverse stick, it must be retrieved by the same player and passed on form his designated position on the circle line.

Variation: The game can be played with two or more balls. Only when all the balls have returned to the original players shall a halt be called.

3.a) Two players stand opposite each other two yards apart. Each then moves three paces to his left. One player is given a ball which he places centrally in front of his body. Both arms are at full stretch gripping the stick, with the toe pointing down to the ground, so that the back of the left hand points to the left and the back of the right towards his partner. The ball is now pushed, with a firm reverse stick pass, to the other player who stops it on the reverse stick side and also returns the ball with a reverse stick pass.

b) As before. This time, however, before each reverse stick pass is made with the ball stationary, the player moves the ball to and fro a few times, in front of the body, as if dribbling Indian style (e.g. forehand-reverse stick-forehand-reverse stick pass).

4. Two players stand facing each other, ten yards apart. One pushes the ball so accurately to his partner that it travels along the line of the partner's left foot. The player waiting for the ball stands facing it at first but, when he is sure that the ball really is coming to him on the left hand side, he turns is body through 90 to the left. To carry out this turn, the player has to pivot round on the ball of his right foot, and the left foot is placed behind the right, so that they are a shoulder's width apart. When in this position the player's right shoulder should be pointing at the passer. This quarter turn of the body is accompanied by a turn of the stick either with the left hand or with the right. The ball is stopped level with the left foot. After the reverse stick stop, the ball can then be taken right round the body, with the player turning to adopt a side-on position facing to the right before pushing the ball back from the normal side on position.

Drills for practising the reverse stick stop on the run:

1. Player no. 1 gives a square pass to the left for player no. 2 to run onto; the latter must stop the ball in one of the following ways depending on the speed of the pass or the speed of his own approach to the ball. If he reaches the ball easily, he makes an orthodox stop, with his feet in the striding position.

   If he is unable to get his body into the line of the ball, he must stop it on the reverse stick, either with two hands or with one hand only, depending on how far he is from the ball. When player no. 2 has definitely got the ball under control, he returns it to player no. 3, who is standing on his right, with a normal pass if he has stopped it normally and with a reverse stick pass, if he had taken it on the reverse stick side. After giving his return pass each player goes to the back of the other group.

2. The first player gives a square pass for player no. 2 to run onto and which the latter stops on the reverse stick. The moment no. 2 makes contact with the ball, player no. 3 runs forward to take the square pass given by no. 2. After giving their passes, players nos. 1 and 2 run diagonally across to the other group and join on at the back. There should be about six to eight yards between players nos. 1 and 3 at the beginning of this drill.

Tactical consideration before or whilst taking the ball

In these days of tight marking and covering, attackers can really only gain possession of the ball without causing some infringement or being obstructed when they learn how to detach themselves from the player marking them at the precise moment that the pass intended for him is given.

The ability to know when to run towards the ball is an important tactical requirement which is still too little heeded in hockey today. Players are usually inclined to wait for the ball to come to them rather than run towards it. Although forwards, above all, have seen enough times how difficult they can make defence for their opponents if only they try running towards the ball, they nonetheless adopt a largely passive role when taking the ball is a great tactical mistake, as it is always much more difficult for a defender to stop a forward already in possession than it is when meeting him at the moment that he is trying to take the ball.

Account must also be taken of the psychological impact which the attacker's self-confidence and sureness in stopping will rise in the same measure as the defender becomes more nervous and unsure, because the forward, by running to meet the ball, prevents the defender from coming into direct contact with it. If the forward waits passively for the ball to come to him, however, then he can be taken by his opponent at just the right moment. Therefore, when a player aims to stop a ball to the side of his body, he should run to meet the ball. Through constant practice, this will become an automatic reaction; beginners should be encouraged to do so form the outset.

Methodical series of drills:

1. Two players stand twenty yards apart behind a marked out line and hit the ball to each other. Immediately before he takes the ball, the player receiving must run towards another line some four to five yards away from him. From here he returns the ball to his partner and then sprints back to his original position. Thus the ball during this practice will always be confined to the space between the inner lines.

2. The first drill can also be carried out with the addition of defenders, who place themselves two or thee yards behind each of the passers. Their job is to challenge their man when he is taking the ball in a side position but not activity to interfere with him.

3. As in 2, except that now both players, a forward and defender, stand on the edge of the circle and, when a pass is given by a third player, from the centre line, they both participate actively. While the

forward tries to gain possession of the ball by running towards it, taking care not to infringe any rule, and then get past the defender into the circle, the defender's job is to pass the ball back to the third player on the centre line, before the forward can touch it.

Stopping by hand on the ground

The handstop is frequently used at short corner. A stickstop for a ball hit out to the edge of the circle is therefore avoided by many sides on flat pitches, because a corner, with a specialist handstopper and a crackshot at goal, can be taken much more quickly, more accurately and therefore more successfully. The corner-taker, who no longer needs to concentrate on stopping the ball with the stick, can devote his undivided attention to the shot at goal; now he can take up the correct position in relation to the ball even before the beginning of the shot and, above all, he can make a short approach run to the ball in order to increase the force of his shot. The handstop, like the stickstop, requires the player to run quickly into position, especially when the pass in inaccurate. At a corner the handstopper must be alert and position himself so that he is always well balanced, one foot in front of the other, directly facing the oncoming ball. The best way to stop the ball is with the fingers pointing downwards towards the stopper's own feet. If the stopper attempts to take hold of the ball from above, however, with the hand merely pressing the ball against the ground, it is all too possible for the ball to roll on under the hand and forearm. A further disadvantage of this type of handstop is that the player has to bend his knees more, with the result that he is less mobile. Moreover, the stopping hand in this method can move relatively little. If the fingers point downwards during the stop and not upwards, the hand can then be moved more easily from the wrist in the direction of the ball and it is far less stiff. The range of movement from the wrist is now greater, which is important when trying to stop bouncing or inaccurately hit balls. When the ball touches the palm of the hand, the fingers must enclose it for a fraction of a second to bring it to rest. Directly after releasing the fingers from the ball, the handstopper should take a pace or two to the side.

A corner taken from the opponent's right hand side is generally easier for the handstopper to stop and for the corner-taker to convert, than one taken from the left; during the latter the handstopper, on the corner-taker's right, has to let the ball run past his body in any case and then stop with the left hand, so as not to get in the way of the shot.

If the shot at goal comes from the inside left position, the handstopper is recommended to stop the ball with left hand beside the right foot, which is advanced, while holding his stick in the right hand. In this way the can use the stick for stopping any ball hit too far to the right which he is unable to reach by running quickly into position. If there is no player in the side who can stop the ball cleanly with the left hand, it can also be stopped with the right hand in front of the left foot, which is advanced in this case. The disadvantages of stopping with the right hand is that the left side of the handstopper's body is now between the ball and the corner-taker, whereas the way to the ball is left clearer when the stop is made with the left hand.

Correct handstopping of the ball on the ground requires more training and skill than the stickstop, above all when the advice already given about stopping with the stick-i.e. to run towards the ball-is heeded. If the handstopper, at a short corner, runs a few paces into the circle immediately after the ball is hit or pushed out, he allows the player taking the corner to shoot from only nine or ten yards but, instead of from the edge of the circle. The chances of scoring a goal are increased, as the reaction time for the goalkeeper and the two defenders standing on the goal-line is reduced and, in addition, the corner-taker is given much more favourable angle for his shot. With a rapid and smooth combination between pusher-out, handstopper and corner-taker (the time from push-out to hit being between 1.5 and 1.8 seconds), the defence is given very little chance, because of the time lost in starting, of reaching the ball in time, as they rush out.

The hit

The hit can often be of decisive importance in the outcome of a match and therefore the coach should concentrate on perfecting it. It is one of the most useful technical acquisitions for any player, of equal importance for both defenders and forwards. Its great advantage over the push and the flick lies in its endless possibilities for moving the ball quickly to any part of the pitch. The hit is made up of several components but a clear distinction is difficult between them as the hit results from a connected series of movements. In theory, the following points are of importance for carrying out a hit successfully:—

1. The position of the player in relation to the ball.
2. The grip

3. The backswing
4. The hit itself

Basically, these for points must be put into practice whenever a hit is made, irrespective of whether it is made from a stationary position or on the run.

Position of the player in relation to the ball

The very fact of adopting a side-on position brings together a series of factors, which are essential for a successful hit, namely:

a) *A firm platform:* The player stands with legs comfortably apart, the left shoulder pointing in the direction in which the ball is to be hit. The weight is placed equally on both feet. One must constantly check that the feet are not too close together, as near as possible to a shoulder's width apart; the feet must be firmly based in order to ensure that the player does not lose his balance while making the hit. A position with the feet any further action is more difficult.

   With a front on position, the platform is less firm, as only the heels support the backwards thrust of the backswing and then of the actual impact, instead of having the whole of both feet as a firm base.

   When the side-on position is adopted, the toes do not point in the direction and to allow the weight to be transferred more easily, the toes point forwards in the same direction as the body.

b) A considerable transfer of weight from one foot to the other is made possible at the moment of impact.

When the front-on position is adopted, there in only a very slight transfer of weight from one foot to the other and therefore it is hardly possible to get any force into the hit.

c) A long backswing is made possible. If the player adopts a front on position the distance travelled by the backswing and the downswing is shorter than when hitting from a side-on position, so that the hit must be less powerful.

   In addition, the left arm cannot be extended fully in the front on position so that full power cannot be transferred to the ball.

d) *The best position visually for the ball:* This is afforded only by a side-on stance. When struck, the ball should be at a comfortable distance from the body, at a point between a line drawn through the centre of the body and the left foot. If the ball is level with the right foot, it is usually chopped ; if it is in front of the left foot, a sliced shot results.

e) *The possibility of disguising the direction of the hit:* For the above reasons, the player should adopt a side-on stance. The closer the player comes to a front-on stance, the more the advantages of the side-on stance already described are lost.

The grip

As soon as the player has taken up the correct position in relation to the ball, the left hand grips the stick from the left and the right hand from the right. The flat side of the stickhead points to the left and is positioned to the immediate right of the ball.

To impart power to the hit, both hands must be

together on the stick one below the other, in direct contrast with the dribbling position. They should be so close to one another, that the index-finger of the upper or left hand should almost touch the littler finger of the right or lower hand. There are two possible positions on the handle for this grip:

a) The right hand, which, grips the middle of the stick in dribbling, slides upwards until it touches the left, or upper hand. This grip is preferred especially by European players, whilst the Asians generally prefer an alternative grip.

b) The Asians slide the left hand down the handle, until it touches the right hand which has been moved about four inches up the handle out of the dribbling position. In contrast to the first position, therefore, the upper four inches of the handle remain free. As there is now a shorter grip on the stick, there is a shorter backswing. In view of this grip's disadvantages, this one advantage is of no real importance. Although the hit can now be carried out more quickly, because of the smaller are described by the stickhead, the downswing in fact must be slower than it is when using the normal grip which permits a greater speed of the stickhead. Because of the shorter backswing, there is less power in the hit. This type of grip in no way avoids sticks, as some Asians believe. On the contrary,, the Asian grip, because it slows down the stickhead, often leads to sticks.

When they first pick up a hockey stick, many people grasp the end of the handle with their right hand, leaving the left hand to grip below the right. Telling a beginner that the world's best players grip the stick with the left hand uppermost, and that he must do likewise if he is to become a good player will not necessarily convince him; even a demonstration may not do so. Only a through explanation will convince him of the disadvantages of his right-hand-uppermost grip, and cause him to change it.

If the stick is held with the right hand at the top of the handle, neither right nor left arm can bend sufficiently to give optimal application of power. The arm muscles are most efficient when the arms are half bent, when muscles are neither over-stretched or over-compressed. With a normal grip, the right hand, being further from the body, does the main work as regards direction and power; the left is simply 'supporting'. If the right hand is gripping the end of the stick, it is drawn in towards the body, and is so fully bent that an optimal transfer of power is impossible. Using that grip, a player cannot hit the ball as hard as he could with the correct grip. Another disadvantage of having the right are drawn in to the body is that it has less freedom of movement, and directional control is much more difficult.

The backswing

At the final point of the backswing, the stick is held as if it were an extension from the right shoulder, so that the tip points upwards. The face does not point to the ground, but is held vertically. If this is not the case, then the stickhead should be brought to a vertical position, at least until the moment of impact, in order to avoid slicing or chopping the hit. At the final point of the backswing, the stickhead should be higher than the grip of the upper hand. In order to achieve this, the right hand must move slightly, thumb upwards. Both wrists are held firm. It must be emphasised that a hit is not produced solely by the action of the wrists, but depends mainly on the arms and the upper part of the body.

Because the arms play such an important part in giving speed to the stickhead and therefore in imparting power to the shot, they must remain free to move. They must not touch the body either during the backswing or at the actual moment of contact. During the backswing the right arm is slightly bent, in contrast to the left. The upper and lower are form an angle of some 102 to 130. The right elbow, as well as the right upper arm, are therefore about a hand's breadth from the ribs. This is a most important point and is ignored by many players.

In the backswing, the stick should never go behind the right shoulder as far to be behind a line extending from the shoulder blade. Therefore, the backswing, together with the ensuing downswing-every movement until the impact-must both be made in the vertical plane.

In order to avoid any checking of the stroke the backswing and the actual downswing should be merged, as far as possible, into one movement. At the final stage of the backswing, the whole weight must be shifted on to the right, or rear, foot.

The hit

The hit itself is started by a shift of weight from the right, or rear, foot on to the left, or front, foot. At the actual moment of contact, both arms are outstretched, the right, however, more so than the left. Fractionally before contact, final acceleration is given to the stickhead by the straightening of the right arm. As far as possible the ball should be struck by that part of the stickhead which touches the grass when dribbling on the right the best place being the middle of the stick's head. If the ball is struck on either side of this area, the stick frequently twists in the player's hand and the ball skews off. From a proper hit struck in the centre of this area, however, the stick remains firmly secure in the player's grip. A hit from the middle of the stick sounds and feels satisfying right.

In order to hit the ball cleanly, the head of the stick must be perpendicular at the point of impact. If the ball is in the wrong position relative to the player, for example too far to the left of the left foot, directly in front to the body, or in front of the right foot, then the head of the stick will be angled either forward or backwards, leading to a chop or a slice. The ball will no longer be struck in the centre.

When a player hits a ball while he is running, he automatically transfers his weight from his right to his left leg, to a greater extent than when he is stationary. Consequently, the position of the ball relative to the player's feet when it is hit, must be altered. When the player is stationary, the point of impact should be B. When he is running, it should be moved beyond the left foot, to A, so as to ensure that the head of the stick is perpendicular to the ball. As a result of this change, the actual movement of the stick in swinging to hit the ball is increased by the distance A-B; this gives the stick more momentum, and greater power. A correct position relative to the ball therefore ensures both greater power. A correct position relative to the ball therefore ensures both greater accuracy and harder hitting a fact which is not sufficiently appreciated in English-speaking hockey-playing countries.

The actual hit begins at point C, after the backswing. The stick pauses here for a moment between backswing and hit, the changes direction rather like a ball just as it starts to fall after being thrown vertically into the air. In order to make it easier to strike the ball, the head of the stick should already be perpendicular to the ground at point C. Accelerate the stick between points C and A; between A and D pay attention to good directional control and avoiding 'sticks'. 'Sticks' after the hit is more common than before; the follow-through by stick and arms is naturally upwards and to the left unless it is checked. Actively holding back the follow-through requires that the tension produced in the muscles during the hit is not released after the impact. In order to hit a ball both technically faultlessly and without infringing the rules, a player needs strength not only for the hit but also for checking the follow-through too.

If the follow-through is accurately in the direction of the hit, then we can generally say that the hit was well executed. But we should note that the important part of a good hit is not just the actual impact, but the backswing, the amount of momentum imparted to the stick, the placing of the stick's face perpendicular to the axis of the ball's travel and the check of the follow-through.

Hitting the ball involves the transfer of weight from the right leg into the left; the whole body is in motion. The movement of the trunk and legs makes the hit more difficult to execute; the movements of the different parts of the body must all be directed towards making the hit. Even more difficult is the hit made when on the move. The player's stick should form an extension of the body and, as the centre of gravity moves up and down in a wavy line because the player is running, so this movement is transferred to the path followed by the stick as it goes to meet the ball.

Most difficult of all, however, is hitting the ball when the action of running has brought the right foot in front of the left at the moment of the hit.

As the point of contact must always vary with a moving ball, and as the player has to modify his positioning each time, the ball, at the moment of contact, should be in the middle of the player's field of vision. Only the best position visually for the ball makes a good hit possible. A good hit and accurate direction are made much easier by keeping the backswing and downswing straight.

Hitting off the wrong foot

It is often impossible for an attacker to hit the ball from the best side-on position with the left foot forward, because he is being closely marked or about to be tackled. If there is insufficient time to bring the left foot forward and turn the body through 90 to the right, a hit off the wrong foot may be necessary. This is made front-on to the ball, despite the dis-advantages this entails. Shoulders and hips do not move in unison as is the case when hitting off the left foot, but form a right angle during the backswing. There is then a sharp twisting of the body between hips and shoulders.

When preparing to hit off the wrong foot, the

player straightens up only a little, and turns his shoulders 90 to the right whilst raising the stick. The left shoulder thus points where he wants the ball to go. As the right foot comes down, the ball is hit from a position in front of and slightly to the side of that foot.

A clean and accurate hit of the wrong foot is achieved by keeping an upright stance during both backswing and hit.

Hitting the ball on the run

Hitting the ball from a run has some advantages over hitting the ball whilst stationary. When the player is running, body and stick act in unison, so that acceleration of the body is transferred to the stick. The faster a player can run towards the ball, the more the stick will be accelerated, and thus the greater will be the strength of the hit.

Hitting the ball in a technically perfect way whilst running is not, however, simple. During the run-up, the stick must be positioned so as to maximise the transfer of power from body and arms to the ball. Usually the stick is raised for the hit quickly, during the penultimate step of the run-up; this reduces the player's speed. He loses further momentum because of the 90 turn to the right and in putting his feet square to the direction of movement. body and stick therefore need to have gained speed early in the run-up; acceleration during the last few steps of the run-up is very slow indeed. The snag is that the faster a player's run-up to the ball, the less time he leaves himself for the backswing and the hit itself. So not only is the technique of hitting the ball complicated, but the chances of scoring a goal are reduced in that the stick has less time to build up momentum, and the hit cannot be as hard. Any increase in run-up speed requires a corresponding improvement in technique. An intelligent corner-striker will not approach the ball at his top speed, but rather at a compromise, medium speed. In so doing, he gives himself sufficient time to give the stick as much momentum as possible from the backswing. Reducing the speed of approach also gives him more time to take up a correct position relative to the hand-stopped ball, and hit it more accurately.

The reverse-stick hit

the reverse-stick hit is a form of hitting off the wrong foot, with the stick held reversed. The closer the ball is to the body in front of the right foot, the easier and harder the ball can be hit; if the ball is too far in front of the body, the stick's head has to be angled too greatly, and the hit can only be executed with the tip of the stick, with a consequent poor transfer of power. If the ball is close to the body, a hard hit with the middle of stick's head is possible, because of perpendicular position of the stick. The grip of the stick remains the same as when hitting on the open side. Over distances greater than about eleven yards, the reverse-stick hit should be used only on very fast surfaces such as artificial turf. On wet grass or other slow pitches, players should also preferentially pull the ball back with reverse stick (rather than *hit*) if under pressure, or hit the ball on the run after, of course, turning the left shoulder in the direction of the intended hit.

Methodical series of drills: from hitting the ball when stationary to hitting the ball at speed.

1. The stationary player hits a ball at rest paying strict attention to the technical suggestions already made.

2. Two players hit the ball to each other. The one receiving indicates to his partner, by the stance he adopts, exactly where he would like to receive the ball to be hit.
3. Groups of three players are formed. The first of two of them standing behind one another hits the ball to a third, who accepts the pass about 20 yards away ; after each player has hit the ball, he runs to the other side, whilst the next player takes his place.
4. The ball is placed in front of the right foot, from where it is slowly propelled to a point about midway between the feet, and while still rolling, is hit towards the other player.
5. From the side-on position, the ball is pushed towards the left past the left foot in the direction of the intended hit. The player overtakes it with a chain step and, at the moment that the left foot comes to the ground again for the second time, the ball is hit to the player.
6. To learn to hit when running, the ball must be hit four to six yards forwards by the player himself. Running quickly after the ball, the player has to carry out a cross-step, immediately before the hit, in order to change from the frontal position to the necessary side-on position; only when the left foot is forward can he then hit the ball to his partner.
7. Relay Practice: The first player dribbles the ball from the centre line to the twenty-five yards line. After running round a flag planted there, he hits the ball back to the next player in the line. If the hit is so weak that the ball does not reach the line of

players, it must be hit again by the same players who has had a run after it. In no case may the player waiting to receive the ball go into the area between the centre and twenty-five yards line before the ball has crossed this boundary.

8. Hitting as in 5 and 6 above. This time the right foot, instead of the left, must be brought forward at the moment that the ball is hit.

9. The above drills 4,5 and 8 can be made more difficult by making two players hit the ball to each other along a straight line or through a narrow goal, made up of two flags, or along a path marked out by two parallel lines. During each drill care must be taken to check that the player's execution of the hit is completely correct.

10. a) Four flags are set up to form two goals, which are each one yard wide, twenty yards apart. All four flags stand on the same line. Ten yards behind one goal are two players. A received a ball and dribbles it, keeping parallel to the line on which all four flags stand; when he is opposite the other goal, he hits the ball over ten yards, while still on the run, through the goal to a third waiting player C. The latter sets off in the same way as A. Having shot the ball through the goal, the player concerned must always run after the ball, so as to take up his new position about ten yards behind the goal, where he waits to receive the next player's shot.

    In the course of the relay practice, all three players act as outside-lefts and practise the very difficult hit on the run over to the right. Those players with little practice at this may be allowed to stop the ball briefly with the reverse stick before hitting to the right, whereas and more adept must hit through the goal while still on the run but without stopping the ball first.

b) If the practice is carried out with four players, two of them can set off simultaneously, each with a ball, so as to rise the tempo of the practice. It is also possible for five players to participate.

c) When only two players are available to take part, the drill is at its simplest. When player A has completed his dribble and hit the ball through the goal, he has to retrace his steps at full speed to get into position behind the second goal and wait for his partner's pass. Who will be the first to score ten goals? If there is too great a disparity between the two players, the size of the goals can be altered in relation to the respective abilities of the participants.

11. Player no. I in each line starts off dribbling at the same time as his opposite number. When they have both covered two thirds of the distance (about thirty yards) and arrived at a point indicated by a flag, they give a moderately hit square pass (off about twenty yards) for the second player of the other group to run onto. Having hit the ball on the run, the player must join the back of the outer line as quickly as possible. It is important that the player, without the ball, from the opposite group does not begin to run before the player dribbling the ball comes level with the flag. The latter player must ensure that his pass is accurate and well timed.

12. 'Chase the ball': The idea of his game is to hit the ball over the sidelines, playing across the width of the pitch in the area bounded by the centre and twenty-five yards lines. After the coach has tossed up to decide which side has the first hit, the game begins with a hit from the side-line. Where the ball is finally stopped by the opponents is the point from which the next hit is taken in the opposite direction. The two sides, four to six players strong, place themselves as suitably as possible in their own half of the playing area so as to be in the best positions to intercept the ball.

    If the ball goes out (i.e. over the centre or twenty-five yards lines), it must be hit back into play by the opposing side at the spot where it crossed the line.

    So that all the players are brought into the game, no player may hit the ball back twice running.

    To decide which is the winning side, either one counts the number of points scored in a specified number of points has been reached.

    Further drills for the hit-shots at goal-are to be found in the chapter on the goalkeeper.

The force of the hit

For the ball to be hit properly certain requirements must be met. In the first place the ball must be struck accurately to reach its target. The player must, therefore, master the technique of producing a clean hit both when stationary and when on the run. Apart from the accuracy of the hit, the force with which the ball is hit must correspond to the player's tactical intentions. In order to be able to import considerable speed to the ball, for example, when shooting at goal, the player should be aware of factors which determine the force of the hit.

The force of the hit depends on the following factors, quite apart from correctness of technique:

1. The player's approach speed.
2. The speed of the downswing.
3. The application of body weight.
4. The hardness of the ball.
5. The approach speed of the ball.

Let us consider these factors separately:

The player's approach

The force with which the ball is struck increases in proportion to the speed at which the player himself approaches the ball for the hit. The impetus gained from the approach increases the power which is applied to the ball. This fact is not sufficiently heeded by many players; otherwise they would no longer take a stationary shot at goal after a handstopped corner or after a short, slow approach to the ball.

Speed of the downswing

The further back the stick is taken, the greater is the acceleration which can be give to the stick on its now lengthened path to the ball. Therefore for a hard hit, not only the player's approach speed is of importance but also the extent of the backswing and, with it, the speed at which the stickhead meets the ball.

The acceleration of the stick must be such that it reaches its maximum speed at the moment of impact with the ball. But in order to achieve considerable speed for the stickhead at the moment of impact, after a relatively short backswing, great force is necessary. The greater the degree of development of the resilience of the player's muscles in relation to his body weight, the easier it is to move the arms an stick quickly. As women are less muscular than men, they are unable to move their arms as quickly and therefore cannot hit as hard as men.

Application of body weight

The weight of the body must not be overlooked when hitting the ball hard. Since the tightly gripping hands from a connecting link between the stick and the body, it is impossible for the weight of the stick alone to be effective in producing the force needed for the hit, and inevitably part of the player's body weight is involved. How much of the player's weight can be brought into play during the hit, depends upon the degree of muscular tension. At the moment of impact, all the muscles involved in the movement of the downswing must be fully tensed, in order to make a really hard hit possible. If, for example, you make a hit with the wrists held slack you will never achieve maximum force, because the firmness of the connecting link between stick and body has been relaxed, with the result that the effect of the body weight is lost. A whippy, yielding stick, too, counteracts the advantages gained by good muscle tension, reducing the force of the hit.

The degree of muscular tension that can be brought to bear at the moment of impact depends on the player's muscle power, thus the stronger individual uses his body weight to greater advantage. Because women cannot produce the same degree of muscular tension in their arms and trunk as men, since their muscles are weaker, the ball does not come off their stick, even when tightly gripped, with the same velocity. This reduced degree of muscular tension is frequently evidenced among women by a visible shaking of the body at the moment of impact between stick and ball. To sum up, it can be said that a player brought up on a regular programme of power and muscle-resilience training can attain a greater degree of muscular tension at the moment of impact; as a consequence of which, the body weight can be more efficiently applied and so, finally, a harder hit is achieved than is possible with a player who has not yet taken power training into consideration in his training programme.

The hardness of the ball

At the moment of impact, the surface of the ball is very slightly dented. Because of its elasticity, the ball immediately afterwards strives to assume its original shape again. The harder the ball is, the greater the effort the ball makes to do this.

A good example for this is the plastic ball, which is much harder than the customary cork or leather ball, and which rebounds much more rapidly from the stick. Thus it can be hit much harder.

The approach speed of the ball

Considerable extra force can be imparted to the ball by a first time shot at goal, if the ball is coming from the right and rolling relatively smoothly in the circle.

The greater the speed of the approaching ball, the greater is the force of the impact between stick and ball, consequently, the harder the shot becomes; it then also carries a greater element of surprise.

The shot at goal

Every action of the attacking side is directed at getting into the circle and producing a successful shot at the opponent's goal. For young players, especially, the shot at goal is a pleasurable aspect of the game's technique, which they will practise enthusiastically for hours. The duel between forward and goalkeeper fascinates them. Every young player would like to beat the goalkeeper so they take special delight in trying to lift their shots at goal.

The most suitable places for the shot at goal, however, are its two lower corners, especially the left hand corner which the goalie cannot reach with his stick. Shots at goal along the ground are very dangerous for the goalkeeper, because the needs more time to save with his feet than for saving a high ball with the stick or hand. Moreover shots at goal along the ground are more successful than high ones, when the speed of the ball is taken into consideration, for the low ball, which is driven with a greater application of body weight and is not travelling in an are, is much faster.

If the shot at goal does go in the air, however, it is more difficult for the goalie to stop when placed in the upper right hand corner of the goal. This is because the goalie's free hand can be moved more quickly than his right hand which is holding the stick; he would, of course, give away a penalty stroke if he were to raise that above his shoulder.

Before the forward shoots at goal, he should be

able to note out of the corner of his eye in a fraction of a second the position, not only goalie, but also the position of the backs. If the position of the backs is such that there is no gap at all for the shot or if only a very unfavourable angle is left, then the forward should look for the chance of passing to a better placed team-mate.

Generally speaking the shot at goal should be made as soon as the forward has crossed the edge of the circle. For this reason all forwards must be able to shoot hard and quickly at top speed, even when the right foot is forwards at the moment of shooting.

As the ball can easily rebound from the goalie's pads or even from the goalposts, the forward should always continue towards goal after getting his shot in to take advantage of any fresh chance of scoring that might arise before the nearest defender can intervene. Many goals are scored in this way, especially from long and short corners. It is not sufficient, though, for only the one player to do this; the other forwards who are in the vicinity of the goal, must also follow up. In order to make this a natural and automatic reaction among the forwards, all practices for shooting at goal should be carried out with a second forward running in with the player shooting at goal and both of them striving to score from the follow-up.

Among advanced players the shot at goal is no longer practised with the player stationary or after dribbling, as it is with the beginners; now it is linked in with other aspects of technique, for example, passing, taking the ball, beating a man and the dummy. By means of practising, at first with passive but later with active opposition, the shot at goal can be carried out almost under match conditions. To give the goalie some interest in the competition, this practice in shooting at goal can also be carried out under match conditions. For coaching, as well as for psychological reasons, group practice is to be preferred to practice between individuals. Which team scores the most goals within a specified period of time? Which team is the first to get ten (fifteen) shots on target? Which team achieves the lowest number of shots off target? To obtain maximum success in these contests, the players, in practising shooting at goal, should try to coordinate the force of the hit with accuracy of direction. The greater the distance from goal, the harder the ball must be hit; even a well aimed shot from the edge of the circle can be easily saved if the ball has only been hit softly because the goalkeeper has sufficient time to adjust his position relative to the speed and direction of the ball.

The goalie will have considerably more difficulty, however, in assessing the speed and direction of the ball, if the opponent does not attempt to control the ball before shooting. The first time shot at goal generally comes so hard and unexpectedly that the goalkeeper scarcely manages to react at all.

If the goalie, in order to narrow the angle, runs out to meet the opponent attempting to get his shot in, the forward should feint to shoot at one corner of the goal and, when the goalie has moved that way, he should then put the ball past him on the other side.

During the course of the game countless attacks are mounted. Only very few culminate with a favourable opportunity for a shot at goal. So as not to squander too many chances for a successful shot at goal, the forwards must use these opportunities with especial concentration, at the moment of shooting, determination and produce. Just as important as concentration at the moment of shooting, determination and prudence when aiming, is self-confidence. Those players who trust their shooting power are generally the best. A lack of self-confidence can only have a detrimental effect on the difficult skill of shooting at goal when at top speed.

The penalty corner

One notices time and time again that moderate teams with excellent goalkeepers and a reliable marksman at penalty corners can beat technically superior teams.

The reason for the surprising defeat of the favourites is generally to be found in their poor technique when taking penalty corners. One frequently sees up to a dozen corners wasted because of lack of concentration, careless positioning and too much improvisation in execution. It must be added that the penalty corner is grossly neglected in training especially by club teams. 'Everything will work out all right in the match'—or so it is hoped. Nowadays however, the importance of extensive practice in taking short corners is proved by the fact that in matches, goals from open play becomes rarer and rarer.

For a penalty corner to be taken successfully, certain basic aspects of hockey technique must be mastered.

1. The ball must be hit, or better, pushed, at moderate speed, accurately from the goal line to the edge of the circle. A push is preferable to a hit as the waiting defenders have great difficulty in

estimating the exact moment that the ball is coming out because of the absence of a backswing.

2. The ball must be stopped cleanly and motionless with the hand or the stick.

3. It must be hit as hard as possible at the goal.

The simplicity of these three requirements could give rise to the false conclusion that penalty corners should generally lead to goals. But the opposition, for their part, are doing everything to prevent a short corner from being carried out successfully. It is not that simple to beat a good goalkeeper who is supported by two team-mates on the goal-line and three other defenders, with one shot from the edge of the circle, and the prospects for the goalkeeper of winning this duel are generally fairly good.

Two reliable players at least are needed when taking a penalty corner; if the ball is to be stopped with the hand then three players at least are necessary and one mistake by any of them results in failure.

If the penalty corner is carried out from the left hand side, the ball should also be stopped if possible with the left hand. If the ball is stopped with the right hand it is vital for the hand stopper to move sideways as quickly as possible in order not to get in the way of the striker.

The player taking the corner should not be stationary when shooting but if possible shout hit the ball after a short but rapid approach to it. The player taking the hit must organise his approach so that the left foot comes forward at the moment of striking the ball.

The first requirement in the defence of a corner is to ensure that the line of vision for the goalkeeper and the two backs standing on the goal-line is never obscured; therefore, the fastest player should run out of the left side of the goal towards the corner-striker with the stick held in the right head only, and a second player, who sets off from a position further out to the right, runs out half-way. A third defender, starting out from the left hand goal-post, generally goes out five or six yards, so as to take any ball on the rebound and to clear them from the danger zone with a push. In support of the six players in defence at least two of the forwards should run back from behind the centre-line to the circle as quickly as they are allowed to by the rules to help in the defence.

If the stopper runs far into the circle, and no defender is able to prevent a shot towards goal, the defence should be organised somewhat differently. In this case the goalkeeper has to run out as far as possible towards the handstopper, so as to narrow the angle of the impending shot at goal. The closer he is at the moment the shot is taken, the greater his chances are of making a save. In order to prevent the striker passing to his left or right to another player, the goalkeeper is accompanied out by a defender on both his left and right hand side. A fourth player has to mark the player pushing the ball out, and the fifth and sixth men guard the goal, each one eighteen inches away from a goal post.

Disguising the direction of the hit

To hit the ball accurately and in the direction intended, the player must, of course, first master the technique of hitting. However, if the ball is not hit precisely in the middle, then spin is imparted to it. Balls with spin can therefore occur partly quite unintentionally because of mistakes in technique. But situations quite often occur during the game in which the use of such a technique can well be advisable for tactical reasons. Balls which are intentionally sliced and which hence give a misleading idea as to the direction the hit finally takes, can only be produced by players of the highest technical and tactical ability.

Before the player learns to disguise the direction of his hitting, he should first of all master two simpler methods for deceiving his opponent. The first is to avoid looking in the direction along which the ball is to be hit. The second method is to take up a misleading stance in order to deceive the opponent and not until the backswing is the left shoulder brought round into the different direction along which the ball will actually travel. For instance the centre half, standing with the ball on the twenty-five yards line, wants to send a free hit to his centre forward. In order to deceive his opponents he places himself so that his left shoulder points towards his outside left or outside right. By means of a quick turn during the backswing, he brings his left shoulder round into the direction of the centre forward who finally receives the ball.

For learning how to disguise the direction of a hit to the left, the player must take up the side-on position to the ball. From this position the ball can be hit without great difficulty in such a way that the opponent cannot anticipate its direction. by maintaining the player's normal position *vis-a-vis* the ball, it becomes possible to alter the direction of the hit at the very last moment. For a clearer understanding of this, an example must be added. If, while taking a free hit, the centre-half stands side-on, pointing in the direction of the outside right, the opposition will try to interpret his intentions from the position he adopts and they will concentrate therefore on the direction that they anticipate the ball will take. A hit to the centre forward or to the inside right when made with this stance, especially when it comes right at the end of the downsizing, is therefore, extremely unlikely. For this reason, and because of the technical difficulties inherent in it, this particular hit can only be mastered by a very few top class players. The centre half has noticed out of the corner of his eye where his opponents have played themselves in anticipation of the hit. As already mentioned, he first of all swings back the stick down towards the ball in the line along which his left shoulder is also pointing. Only at the very last second, directly before the stickhead meets the ball just to the right of middle, the player, using his right wrist, turns the stick slightly towards the left, and with the stickface slightly tilted towards the left, the hit is carried out in a different direction, i.e. towards the centre forward. To make this hit to left easier, the ball should lie further than is otherwise normal in front of the left foot.

If, in order to disguise the direction of hit made to the left, the ball has to be struck to the right of the centre, then conversely if force is applied to the ball to the left of the centre, a hit to the right will result. And the further the ball is hit to the side, the more it will deviate sideways from the anticipated straight line.

When the intention is to disguise the direction of a hit made to the right, as in this latter example, the player must stand far enough away from the ball for the stick to swing freely in its arc between the right leg and the ball. It can then strike the ball to the left of centre on that face of the ball which is pointing directly towards the right foot. The disguised hit to the right varies in many respects from the normal hit, the most important of which are :

1. The position of the stick face relative to the ball is, at the moment of impact, quite different. In this case the ball is not hit centrally but to the side of its mid-point.
2. Striking the ball is rendered more difficult because of the smaller striking surface.
3. The ball is sliced rather than hit. To achieve this, the area of the stick face between the centre of the curve and the toe is made to slide round the ball by giving it a slight turn to the left with the right wrist, so that the palm of the right hand is pointing slightly upwards. Because of this slice the ball will travel more slowly than one which has been hit dead centre even though the speed of the hit is the same. The reason for this is that the full weight of the hit cannot be transmitted to the ball. It is also much more difficult to calculate accurately the force of a disguised hit.
4. One of the most important features of the disguised hit to the right is the change in the direction of the hit at the very last moment.

One sees the disguised hit to the left more frequently in a match than the disguised hit to the right. One sees the latter used especially when a free hit is taken immediately outside the opponent's circle.

The centre half, for example, position himself in such a way that is left shoulder is pointing towards his inside left. Neither his pick-up nor the actual downswing give any indication at first of any different direction for the free hit to take than to his inside forward.

Only at the very end of the downswing, without any alteration in the player's stance, is the ball heavily sliced by means of the change in the position of the stickhead and a change in position of the point of impact, so that the ball skews off abruptly into an open space in the direction of the centre forward.

Practice drills to encourage the use of the disguised hit and to help improve its technical application under match conditions.

1. Two teams each with three players line up opposite each other about twenty yards apart, across the width of the normal hockey pitch. A third team with two or three players takes up its position in the middle between the other two sides. The two outside teams now attempt to pass the ball to each other through the gaps in the middle team, while the players in the middle strive to prevent them. The players in the outside teams are allowed to pass the ball among themselves so as to find a favourable opportunity for a pass through the middle.

2. Two teams with six players in each are divided up into two equal groups. The groups take up their positions on the pitch. Team A occupies areas I and 3, Team B areas 2 and 4. The players attempt to get the ball through to the other group of their own players, so that the players in the middle cannot

intercept the pass which must not rise above knee level. This practice takes place on a normal hockey pitch. The winning team is the one to achieve the most passes within the certain time.

3. "Spy in the Camp': Two teams each with three players are separated from each other by a neutral strip six to eight yards wide. Each group send one man (the fourth player) into the enemy camp. His own team-mates attempt to pass the ball to this spy. If they succeed, the player who passed the ball changes over into the enemy camp as a second spy. Which side will get all its men as spies into the opponents' camp first?
4. 'Chase the Ball': Three against three on the whole field.

8

THE DEFENCE

Defence is first and foremost the job of the backs and halves. But the forwards, too, must frequently play their part in defence. Their primary defensive task should always be to hinder the opposing defence, at least at the moment that they are trying to take the ball. A forward who fails to do this and who stands around after losing the ball. A forward who fails to do this who stands around after losing the ball or after a shot at goal, is tactically immature. Not only backs and halves but forwards as well must be coached in the technique and tactics of defence.

In contrast to the forwards, the most important task of the defence is to prevent goals from being scored by the opposition. The main difference in difficulty between attacking and defensive play lies in the fact that a player, when attacking, can usually determine his own moves, whereas the defender has to adapt his to the opposing forward and react corresponding to his movements and actions.

But to be able to react correspondingly, the defender must not remain completely still for a angle moment in defence. He must constantly be on the move, well balanced, always shifting his weight rapidly from one leg to the corner. Correctly timed defensive actions, such as swift lunges towards the opponent with the ball, in any direction, forwards, to the side and even quickly backwards, are then much easier to produce. Apart from a certain mobility and agility, the defender requires, above all, the ability to size up the overall situation and rapid powers of decision. When the opposing side is in possession, a well trained defender will always keep a close eye on the ball and his opposite number, so as to be able take him at the correct moment, to intercept a pass or be able to prevent his opponent from running into an open space behind his back. Rapid awareness of the defensive possibilities as they crop up, as well as the ability to give orders speedily for the appropriate move to be carried out, depend, to a great extent, on the player's capacity to grasp the situation and make a rapid decision.

Good covering is an important factor for morale, especially when a team is playing away or against very strong opposition. The feeling of safety and confidence in the team's covering benefits the forwards and gives them fresh encouragement.

Psychological reasons speak in favour of the defender taking good care to see that his first contact with the ball is as successful as possible. That gives him great personal self-confidence. If, at the first encounter, the defender meets his man in a hard and determined way, the attacker at the next encounter will, under certain circumstances, be already a little inhibited and the prospects of success for the defender will be substantially increased.

Effective cover, which imbues the side with spirit and self confidence, is dependent as much on the performance of individual players as on co-operation between all the members of the side. Without mutual support and assistance no defence today can expect success. Before the members of the defence learn how to support each other, they must first achieve mastery over the individual principles of defence. These include:

1. Positional play.
2. Lunging forward to tackle
3. Tackling in retreat
4. Worrying the opponent when taking the ball.
5. The close marking of an opponent
6. Extending the defender's reach.

Positional play

In principle, the defender should stand between his opponent and his own goal on an imaginary straight line running from the attacker to the middle of his goal.

He can in certain situations, deviate from this theoretical line, when, for example, the ball is on the opposite side of the field. Then the defender should move a little away from the imaginary line, towards the middle in the direction of the ball. Such a change of position makes it possible for the defender who has moved inwards, to be able to assist his colleague more quickly and more easily if he is beaten. Since the defender, however has always sufficient time, if there is a pass to the right, to cover the opponent entrusted to his charge, this change in position represents no risk at all.

One cannot make a generally valid statement as to the distance to be left between the defender and the forward being marked. That depends on several factors.

1. On the speed of the opposing forward and on the speed of the defender. If the defender is faster than the forward, he can stand quite close to him. A slower defender, however, should place himself three to four yards away from the forward.

2. On the technical ability of the opponent. If the attacker has a good technique but is slow, the defender then stays closer to him, so that the mere presence of the defender will put the forward off as he receives the ball. If the forward's technique is clumsy however, the man marking him can stand at a greater distance.

3. On the player's position on the pitch. If the attacker is a long way away from his opponent's goal, the defender can happily remain six yards or more away from him. But the closer the forward comes to goal, the more dangerous he is and the more closely he must be marked.

A very important condition in positional play is that the defender should keep his opponent constantly in front of him and yet, at the same time, keep an eye on the ball. This two-fold task can only be avoided if the defender has learnt how to look both directly and out of the corner of his eye. Correct positioning is, of course, a most important aspect of defence but is not sufficient in itself to repulse the opponents' assault.

Lunging forward to tackle

Lunging forward to challenge is the commonest form

of tackling, and is particularly successful if the opponent does not have the ball fully under his control-for instance if he has let the ball roll too far away from him stick whilst dribbling.

The lunge should start from the 'basic defensive position' in which the player's weight is equally distributed on both feet. This enables him to make quick defensive reactions in any required direction. When the lunge tackle is off the left foot, the left hand flings the stick powerfully towards the ball. By putting his left foot forward, the defender can increase his reach; another benefit of reaching out as far as possible is that if the first lunge should fail, the tackler can try again by stepping back with his left foot: he will not have to turn round, if his reaction to failure the first time is quick enough. If the lunge is made off the right foot, then not only is his reach impaired, but his view of play is restricted, since his upper torso is necessarily bent forward more than if the lunge were off the left foot. This restricted vision can easily lead to collisions with other players. In contrast to the left shoulder, the right should always be kept well away from the ball.

Methodical series of drills for coaching the lunge tackle.

1. *Lunge tackle without a partner.*

   Players individually practise the defensive lunge off the left foot, at a ball lying about three yards in front of them. They should practise both starting from the basic position, and after 'dancing on their toes".

2. *Lunge tackle with a partner.*

   Two players stand facing each other about six yards apart, and lunge towards each other simultaneously, in order to test each other's reach : the ball remains motionless between them. Watch for technical accuracy in carrying out the lunge tackle.

3. *Lunge tackle with a partner ; competitive practice.*

   On a signal from the coach, two players both lunge tackle at the ball placed midway between them. The aim is to touch the ball first. If the right hand keeps hold of the stick, then an otherwise-successful attempt should not count. The winner should be the first to five. In order to be make the lunge as quickly as possible, the player should fling his stick immediately towards the ball, with the stick starting from a horizontal position ; there should be no preparatory 'winding up'.

4. *Defensive lunge will a partner, but without the ball.*

   Each player has to try to touch his partner's foot with his stick.

5. *Defending against a passive forward dribbling the ball.*

   In order to avoid injuries due to lunge tackles hitting the shins and feet, forwards should dribble the ball straight in front of the body, close to the stick. When the forward comes within reach of the tackler, the latter lunges forward from a position a little to the left of his opponent, rather than from immediately in front. Such a side on position increases the arc through which the tackler has opportunities to gain possession of the ball. If the tackler succeeds, then he should transfer all his weight onto his left foot and try to bring the deflected ball under control within a few paces. If he fails in the tackle, he should retract his front foot, in order to have a second chance to gain possession.

6. *As in 5., but with a preceding body swerve or stick feint.*
7. *As in 5., but with or without preceding feints.*
8. *As in 5., but with a delayed tackle.*

   In the case, the defender tackles only when the forward's ball is level with him (the defender). Active dribbling by the forward, with sudden changes of direction, is not allowed, since his role is passive. He should always control the ball close to the curve of the stick.

9. *Lunge tackle as a competition.*

   Any number of players dribble a ball inside a limited area. Each player has to try to hit the balls of other players out of the playing area, using lunge tackles, without losing control of his own ball. The last player still dribbling his own ball is the winner. If a player loses his ball, he goes into an adjoining area where a separate competition is held for those knocked out first.

Tackling in retreat

The lunge tackle should be used by a defender only when the attacker has allowed the ball to roll too far away from his stick whilst dribbling. If the forward has full control of his ball all the time, this type of tackle is recommended: a forward having close control of the ball would have little difficulty in beating the tackle by selling a dummy.

In tackling in retreat, the defender moves out of the forward's path to place himself at his side, thus presenting him with an open space. The players do not confront each other, therefore, but run side by side. The defender continues to shadow the forward thus, until he sees a favourable opportunity for dispossessing him.

The intelligent defender tries to create suitable situations for a successful tackle as he follows the forward back by means of dummy movements with his stick and body. By these means he forces his opponent into making involuntary moves, so that the defender's chances of success in the duel between the two increases. The great advantage of tackling in retreat is that the marker, after an unsuccessful attempt to tackle, has one, two, three, or more further chances, as the forward has not already beaten him. But if, on other hand, the defender lunges forward to tackle from a stationary, frontal position and fails to win the ball, he has then, first of all, to transfer back his weight, which is now well forward, turn round and then start running after a standing start. After all this the forward will be well away.

It is important while tackling in retreat for the defender always to keep his eye on the ball. If he observes this advice, he will never be deceived by a stick dummy or a body swerve into making a false move himself.

1. *Preliminary exercise (shadow running).*

   Two players run without sticks, slowly at first, but later rather more quickly, maintaining a distance of two yards between them. Whereas A run forwards, sideways or backwards at will in an effort to surprise the other player, B has to imitate all these movements in such a way that he constantly maintains the required two yards' distance from his partner.

3. *Shadowing by the defender*

a) The attacker, playing between the twenty-five yards line and the goal line without a stick, tries out various individual attacking movements at moderate speed to try and beat the defender, who meets him face to face but then keeps to his side, to the goal line.

It is defender's task at this stage on the practice to adopt the correct positioning (see 'positional play', page 138) relative to his opponent and prevent his running into the open space. The defender must not actually touch his opponent.

b) As in a) above except that both players now carry their sticks but still without a ball.

c) The practice is further extended in that the attacker is now given a ball but the defender is still not allowed actually to take it away from him, but should, constantly maintain his correct position in relation to the ball and his opponent. In exercise b) and c) the defender should quite intentionally put into effect various defensive dodges to upset the approaching forward. The exercise can be made competitive by seeing who can delay for the longest time a successful attack by an opposing forward.

3. *Talking in retreat*

Two players stand opposite each other, about six yards apart. There is a ball midway between them, and a flag six to eight yards behind each player.

After lunging towards the ball, each player transfers his weight back to the right foot, turns to the right, and tries to be first to touch the flagpost with his stick. At first this exercise should be done only making a right hand turn. Putting too much weight on the front foot in making the lunge tackle will slow down any backward turn in the direction of the flagpost. Each player should therefore try to push off them his left while it is still bent as he turns : this requires that when he touches the ball, his centre of gravity is not quite over the left leg. When he is running back to the flagpost, he should hold the stick only in his left hand.

When he is tackling in retreat using a reverse stick lunge, the defender needs to alter his positioning. Now he had the attacker on his right side, with his own right foot forward. He should hold the stick well in front of his right foot, so as to block the forward's path to his left and force the forward to go to his right (reverse stick) side.

4. *Tackling in retreat against a forward dribbling passively*

   The defender waits for the forward to come towards him, and then moves to one side of the forward's path, letting the forward come level with him on either the open or reverse side. He then shadows the attacker in retreat, after feinting a lunge tackle. As he shadows, he makes further dummy movements with both stick and body. As the defender improves, the passive attacker should increase the speed at which he dribbles.

5. *Tackling in retreat with active defence*

   Playing between the twenty five yards line and the

goal line, the defender now attempts to dispossess the attacker, who constantly alters the direction of his dribbling. If the dribbler succeeds in beating the defender with the ball, and in reaching the goal line before him, the attacker scores one point, just as the defender does, if he succeeds in winning the ball. After each attempt the positions are reversed. The condition is imposed on the defender at each attempt to tackle that he has to retreat for at least ten yards before the real attempt to tackle is made.

6. *Active defence in a square (fifteen yards square), against active forwards.*

   Five forwards, one after the other, attempt to beat the active defender who tackles in retreat within the square (but who remains in the square the whole time) in such a way that they can dribble the ball across the end line. If the ball goes out of play over a side line or over the other end of the square, or if the defender can dispossess the forward without fouling, then the defender scores one point. If the defender fouls, then the forward has another turn. Each forward has two attempts against the defender. After ten attacks the defender swops places with one of the forwards. Which of the five forwards is the most successful defender?

7. *One against one on a pitch fifteen yards long, with goals ten yards wide.*

   The two players engage each other until one is able to dribble the ball over his opponent's goal line.

After a goal is scored or if the ball goes over the goal line, the two players take a rest. While two reserve players, who have been spectators behind the two goals, carry on with the game, the two players resting go behind the goals, ready to take over again the next time a goal is scored or the ball goes off over again the next time a goal is scored or the ball goes off over the goal line. The new attack is always started from the end at which the last goal was scored or at which the ball went out of play. Thus the opponent of the man in possession is automatically the defender.

Apart from tackling in retreat, which is something mastered by very few players in the world, and some technical and tactical aspect of individual attack, the players can learn two important tactical lessons when the ball is lost ; immediate pursuit of the opponent and the lightning fast switch from defence to attack.

Worrying the opponent when taking the ball

The skilful defender can work out the likely direction of a pass from the movements, the eyes, and the characteristics of the player dribbling. If the defender is unable to intercept the ball by running quickly onto the line of the pass, he should be at least attempt to take the forward by surprise from behind at the moment that he is bringing the ball under control, so as to make the forward obstruct. This frequently occurs in a match, because, in such cases the forward, is directing all his attention to the approaching ball and forgets, therefore to adopt a side on position to the ball and, more important, to run and meet the pass.

Methodical series of drills for worrying the opponent when taking the ball.

1. In the beginning the defenders practise intercepting the ball running swiftly forwards. A player passes the ball from a distance of eight to ten yards to his partner standing opposite, behind whom stands the defender. The defender attempts to pick up the ball

before the proper recipient by running round him and then giving it back to the original passer. The ball should be passed unexpectedly without any obvious preparation. At first the attacker is not to move towards the ball.

2. The practice is made more difficult; the attacker now hinders the defender as he runs forward by moving towards the ball himself in a side-on position.
3. The pass is now made over a distance of twenty, instead of eight to ten yards. Both the defender and the forward now try to reach the approaching ball first. Whoever can return the ball to the passer without fouling, is the winner. Whilst the two players are fighting for possession of the ball, the passer can move into a new position.
4. As a variation, the defender can be instructed not to take the ball away from the forward until the moment that the forward is trying to control the ball.

Close marking an opponent

Worrying an opponent when taking the ball is easiest to do when the defender marks his opposite number closely, and by doing this we mean remaining within his reach. If the defender follows him everywhere he goes, we can talk of marking him out of the game or close marking. The defender directs his attention first and foremost to his opponent and then to the ball, without, however, losing sight of the overall situation.

Close marking an opponent demands that the defender be in peak condition for he has to keep up with his opponent whenever he moves into an open space. However, if the opponent is superior to the defender in speed, perseverance, stamina and agility, then obviously the attempts at marking him out will be unsuccessful. Good foot-work and balance are prerequisites for being able to mark an opponent this closely at all times. It is best practised by simple games involving running and frequent sudden stops and unexpected changes of direction. Training defenders to mark opponent out under match conditions is best undertaken in miniature games with forwards attacking large or small goals.

Learning how to mark a man is very important for developing an individual grounding in defence and it forms the basis for all other types of marking. As the principles of individual defensive play are learned earlier in this way then, for example, in learning how to cover, close marking should be learned first and practised for a long time before moving on to other aspects of marking. Once the players have learned how to mark their man, they will understand much more easily about covering or combined marking. If, on the contrary, covering is introduced first, as used to be the case, then learning to mark a man will entail later difficulty.

If a defender tries to mark a dangerous forward out of the game, he is in no way playing purely defensively. Rather, his marking is designed to aid the attack, reinforcing the need for attacking tactics, because the man in possession is immediately tackled. The defender should never look on passively when his man goes into the thick of the game. Modern defenders, who mark their man tightly and very early, are not playing defensively but are showing that they are naturally attacking.

Graduated series of practice games designed to practise close marking

1.a) *One against one with a neutral passer.*

A mid-field player (link-man) pushes the ball to his forward who is to try and score a goal while being tightly marked by a defender. The free hit must be taken within five seconds. In this period of time, the forward must have got away from his defender, so that he can take the ball without obstructing. For each goal scored by the forward without fouling, the forward and the passer receive one point.

The players change round after ten attacks. The defenders becomes the forwards, the forward becomes the passer and he takes on the defender's position. Who has scored the most points after the thirty attacks?

b) One against one with a neutral passer.

If the defender wins the ball, he changes over to the attack. After the defender has succeeded in passing to the passer, the former forward takes over the defence. Whoever manages to score a goal, can carry on in attack. The passer is not allowed to shoot at goal.

In these and the following exercises, the defender can practise and will improve: marking a forward closely, accurate passing after a successful tackle (while still under pressure from an opponent), the quick changeover from defence to attack and also tackling in retreat, after failing to win the ball from the forward as he was bringing it under control.

The effect of these practices on the forward will be to encourage skilful disengagement by dodging about the variations in speed, taking the ball without obstructing and then using it for dribbling and carrying out dummy moves. The passer learns the correct moment for giving a pass and how to agree certain movements with his forward which can be carried out without misunderstanding.

2.a) *Two against two with a neutral passer (as in I. a) and I. b) above).*

b) Two against two with a neutral passer.

Line-up as in 1.a) above. This time, however, the passer must pass the ball while on the run over at least ten yards, immediately after a slalom round three flags, to one of the two forwards who have become unmarked for a second. While dribbling, the dribbler must look up from the ball, so as to be able to pass to the best-placed player.

c) Two against two with a neutral passer and sweeper.

The passer, from a stationary position, serves one of the forwards who has become unmarked and who, with the assistance of the passer and the second forward, has to try and score a goal against two defenders who are marking and the one sweeper who is covering. The passer, however, may not score goal and should always maintain a distance of eight to ten yards from his forwards. The sweeper behind the defenders cuts off passes from the passer into the gaps and always helps out when one of the defenders is beaten by a forward.

3. a) *Three against three with a neutral passer and sweeper in front of the circle.*

   Line-up as in 2.c) above except that there is now one extra player, both in attack and defence. By means of frequent interchanging of position, the three forwards should try to make close-marking more difficult for the defenders. The defenders should apply close or combined marking.

   b) Four against four, dribbling the ball over the line.

   On losing the ball, three players in the team concentrate on marking their opposite numbers, whereas the fourth acts as sweeper. The side in possession plays with three forwards and one passer, who becomes the sweeper when the ball is lost. Passer and sweeper may not dribble into the opposing half. The game takes place across the width of the field.

   c) Four (three) against four (three) on the goal-keeper Only after at least one pass amongst the player of one side can a goal be scored.

4.a) *Four against four with a passer and sweeper.*

   b) Five against five, dribbling the ball over the

line; four players in the team, losing the ball, must concentrate on marking their opposite numbers, using close or combined markings.

c) Four against four, with two mid-field players, one sweeper and one goal-keeper.

Neither mid-field players is allowed to move upfield beyond the 35 yards line. They can play the ball to each other until one of the four forwards being tightly marked by the opposition has been able to break free.

d) Variation on c). One of the mid-field players may now, occasionally, join in with the attack. By doing this the sweeper is forced to take on the extra man. As the defence is no longer superior in numbers, the remaining four defenders have to give up their marking and change to covering, whereby the two backs (mostly the left) take on the role of backing up the sweeper. The second mid-field player, as previously, should not cross the twenty-five yards line. The mid-field players are not allowed to pass the ball more than three times amongst themselves.

e) Variation on c). If the defence can get the ball into their possession and pass three times among themselves, they score one point; so, too do the forwards (at most, five) if they can touch the ball within the circle. A goal scored counts two points.

f) Variation on c). Counter-attacking allowed.

If a defender gains possession of the ball, he attempts to hit it as quickly as possible through one of two goals, four yards wide, placed on the centre-line in the left wing and right wing positions. Immediately after losing the ball the attacking side must quickly change over to defence, with the four forwards covering the man previously marking them, and the two mid-field players guarding the two goals on the centre-line. The team which first scores twenty points wins.

These methodical practice games guarantee the step by step development of close marking from the individual, through the group to the whole team; they guarantee also that defensive technique and tactics are trained both individually and collectively. From one type of game to the next, the players practising become more capable in summing up in a flash the state of play, of anticipating the most appropriate solution and then carrying it out automatically, whilst the ever-changing situation puts new demands on their tactical thoughts and actions. Apart from considering the position of team-mates, a watch must be kept on the positions, actions and probable intentions of the opponents; above all, the ball must constantly be watched.

Finally, attention must be directed to the fact that sufficient time has to be spent on these drills in training and that, in one week, only one of the 15 various types of game should be introduced for, Otherwise, the introduction of close marking in a game could be a failure.

Extending the defender's reach

A good defender masters not only positional play, the

basic defensive stance, and the various ways of collecting the ball but is also able to put his reach to its best advantage. To control as large an area of the pitch as possible, the player's reach must be improved and extended by training. If the player does learn to extend his reach, he will find it easier when covering, to cut off passes to the loosely marked opponent or when, marking closely, to cut off passes into the gap.

Methodical drills: extending the player's reach

1. Player A faces player B at a distance of four yards. To the right to player B, and level with him, is a flag (three yards away). When A plays the ball in the direction of the flag, B alters his basic stance by executing a quarter turn to the right on the ball of the right foot, and, at the same time, places his left foot well past the right foot. At the end of this sideways lunge, after transferring the outside leg, both feet point towards the flag or towards the ball.

   If the player's reach needs to be extended still further, the stick is then held with the left hand only, and the right hand is released. Only by leaving hold of the stick with the right hand, can the right shoulder be held back, thereby allowing the left shoulder to be pushed further forwards towards the ball. This practice is carried out incorrectly then if player A, in attempting to reach the ball, persists in the basic position and tries to bridge the gap merely by stretching wide his legs but without transferring his outside leg across. In this outstretched and strained position, the defender is left relatively immobile and, after an unsuccessful tackle, is no longer in a position to try and tackle again. Before he can pursue his man, he has to straighten up again, which take time. Had the defender in the picture transferred his left leg past the other towards the right, he would have been able, because the increased reach thus achieved, to adopt a much more favourable position for tackling the forward.

When extending the player's reach on the reverse stick side, the right foot is transferred past the other to the left, at the same time as the player makes a quarter turn towards the left on the left foot, so that, at the moment of stopping the ball with the reverse stick, both feet are pointing in the direction of the ball.

Since the right foot at the moment of stopping is in front of the left, it follows that the left shoulder, in relation to the right, is pushed forwards only slightly. After the reverse-stick stop, which can be carried out in various ways, attention must be paid to see that the back of the left hand points backwards. In contrast to the grip from underneath, with the back of the hand pointing downwards, this grip enables a greater degree of power to be developed.

The practices outlined in 1 and 2 above are best carried out in front of a wall or a fence, because any balls that are missed will immediately bounce back to the passer.

3. Players A,B and C from an equilateral triangle, the sides of which are six yards long. Between B and C, who stand in front of a flag, a defender places himself facing the passer, player A.

   The latter is given a ball and plays it alternately,

first to B and then to C, without in so doing, leaving the triangle. The defender's task is to extend his reach, by transferring the outside leg and pushing forward his left shoulder in such a way that he can pick up the pass to B or C. In the beginning it is always practised in the above sequence, in order to groove the correct footwork. After every ten passes from the player in position A, the players change round in a clockwise direction, that is to say, B takes Ads place and C moves into the triangle to become the defender. Only when the use of a player's reach has been mastered, both to the left and to the right, by all four players, may the passer send the ball in any sequence he cares, to left or to right. After ten passes which defender has picked up the most?

4. The practice described in 3 above can be increased in intensity by doing away with players B and C. The defender now stands in the middle of a goal and, by use of his reach, must prevent passes from player A going through the goal. The defender is allowed to extend his reach slightly by taking a short preliminary step with the nearest leg towards the ball, before transferring the outside leg across.

   Who scores the most goals with pushed passes? This, too, is best practised in front of a wall or fence, so that fetching balls that are missed does not take too much time.

Covering in defence

An important condition for the efficient functioning of the defence as a unit backing up in defence, with the defenders changing places among themselves.

A defence, in which the individual players co-operate well, knows how to lend mutual support, quickly and efficiently, when the opponents have beaten one of its own men. Changing positions in an extremely important weapon in defence and it takes place whenever a forward backs through and is taken on by the player nearest to the beaten defender. The swop in position must be carried out very carefully and prudently. A few examples will show how this swopping of positions in defence must be carried out, with the orthodox line-up of five forwards, three halves and two backs.

The right wing has beaten the left half and is bearing down at goal. What must now be done? So that the attack can be checked, the left back, who is nearest to the LH, leaves his own inside forward and slowly approaches the RW. In doing this he pays close attention to see that the winger does not give a through pass for his IR to run onto. He must attempt to induce the winger, either to engage in time consuming dribbling, or to make an attempt to beat him or to hit a square pass. If the winger dribbles or gives a square pass. If the winger dribbles or gives a square pass, this allows the beaten LH time to take over the marking of the inside forward, who has been left by the LB. The numerical balance is therefore once again restored.

Above all, defenders should guard against leaving their own man too early when swopping positions. If the LB leaves his inside forward immediately to take on the RW as he breaks through, he then runs the risk that the RW will pass the ball immediately to the ER, before the LH has been able to take over marking the IR.

A change of position must take place, therefore, only when the action is between the twenty-five yards line and the defender's own goal line. If for example, the opposition centre forward breaks through, then the nearest of the two backs (generally the left back, who does not have to play the ball on the reverse-stick side) must take on the CF without delay, because the constitutes the greatest danger for the defence. The slightest delay, here, can lead to a goal. In this case, changing positions is carried out without any great difficulty, since the distance from defender to defender and also between the forwards is much less just in front of goal than it is in mid-field.

In coaching how to change positions, the coach should constantly watch out to see that there is always a diagonal line-up in defence. The aim of the diagonal line-up is to facilitate the changing of positions in case of opposition breaks through. As the coach is unable to keep on giving instructions during the course of the game from off the pitch, he should designate a player, who can pass on instructions about correct positional play and about changing positions as it becomes necessary.

Assistance in defence, by means of interchange of positions among defenders, is made easier if a free man is employed in the 4:2:3:1 formation behind the main defenders. This last line of defence, having no special opponent to mark, has the job of coming to the help of the left half, for example, if he is beaten by his right wing, or to the help of the centre half when the opposition centre forward has broken through. In the 4:2:3:1 formation, therefore, this same specialist defender changes position and assists the rest of the defence, so that they can devote their entire attention to marking their men. There are many situations, however, when a back or mid-field player has moved up-fields and has not turned at the correct moment, so that he is no longer able to catch the man he is supposed to be marking; then, an interchange of positions and covering becomes necessary, as described above.

Covering in defence, by means of an interchange of positions among the defenders, used to be discussed mainly only in theory but severely neglected in practice. So as to increase sureness in defence and the self-confidence of the players, it is to recommended, however, that covering by systematically coached with great care, aiming at a certain degree of perfection.

It is frequently occurs that covering is no longer possible. One back is then left to face two attackers. In these circumstances, the back is not necessarily recommended to try to dispossess the dribbler immediately but rather to make as if to tackle him in order to try and force the forward into passing.

This is the moment that the back has the best chance of a successful intervention. The defence gets into such a situation when two defenders are left to face three forwards. The first method is for the two backs to give the impression that they are going to take the dribbler and the player nearest to him; this should cause the dribbler to pass to the furthest away to his two colleagues. However, the second back, who is not directly engaging his man, is waiting for just this pass. A second method is to delay the attack as long as possible by retreating in defence, so that the beaten defender can get back into position. This method, however, applies only in mid-field.

The push stroke

In direct contrast with the hit, the push is mostly used for passing over short distances. Beginners should be instructed in pushing from the very first coaching session, after they have first assimilated the basic principles or dribbling on the right as the push is the quickest and easiest of all the methods of passing to learn.

The complete movement of the push is relatively simple compared with the other ways of passing i.e. the hit, the flick and the scoop. It takes far less time and is carried out without much preliminary action. Using the pushed pass, the player dribbling with the ball can play the ball at any moment in any direction even when dribbling at top speed.

Just as with the hit, the player should place himself sideways-on to the push, as far as is possible, so that his left shoulder points in the intended direction of the pass. The feet are a shoulder's width apart, the legs are well bent, not straight, and the trunk is inclined slightly forwards. The left hand takes hold of the stick from the left or from above, and grips it at the top of the handle, while the right hand is brought round onto the stick from the right and holds it in the middle. The ball is placed midway between the two feet at a comfortable distance in front of the body, with the stick forming an angle of something like 35 to 45 to the ground. Because the face of the stick is placed directly behind the ball, the backswing is dispensed with and so, too, the crack of stick hitting ball is missing on impact.

The push stroke results from an explosive and lightning quick whipping action of the right arm towards the left. The right arm is slightly bent in the initial position, but is at full stretch during the final movement.

However, in order to be in a position to give a good, hard pushed pass, it is absolutely necessary for the player, before pushing, to adopt a side-on position, with feet parallel and apart and the weight firmly placed on the right (or back) foot. Simultaneously with the action of pushing, and to replace the power derived from the pick-up, there takes place a shift of weight from the right foot, which is bent, onto the left foot; in so doing the right leg is straightened because of the quick, powerful thrust as the weight is finally transferred.

At first many players find difficulty in pushing the ball any great distance, because they cannot co-ordinate exactly enough the movement of the arms and the shift to weight from one foot to the other. However, when they do learn to transfer the weight of the body and, at the same time, to apply the muscle power of the arms and the shoulders to the stick, they will certainly be able to push the ball the width of the field.

At the end of the push stroke the stick should follow through after the ball as far as possible, so as so keep better control over it and thus obtain maximum accuracy of direction. If, however, immediately after the shift in weight and the actual push stroke, which are both aimed in the same direction, the direction of the stick face following through after the ball, is swiftly changed to the left or right, the opponent can easily be deceived by thus concealing the direction of the push and will have great difficulty recognising the passer's real intentions.

The push can also be carried out from a frontal position. As it is then not possible to put the weight of the player's body to any real advantage and as the room available for the full use of the arms is also severely restricted, maximum power cannot be developed with a pushed pass made from this position.

Power can only derive from the strength of the forearms and, additionally, from the action of the wrists. Moreover, the pushed pass from a frontal position is generally much less accurate than one from the side-on position, as the position of the body impedes ball control. Despite this, every player should master this pass, particularly as he will not always have the time in a game to get into a side-on position when trying to push to his front.

The pushed pass from the frontal position lends itself especially well to being learnt at the same time as stopping to the front. An example: Two players stand facing each other at a distance of three to four yards and take turns in passing the ball, which is placed between their feet in front of the body. The stick is inclined at about 45 for both the push to the front and stopping to the front, so that the left forearm forms an extension of the stick in a straight line. Should the ball be passed to the opponent's right or left instead to between his feet, the player receiving the ball has to transfer his weight to that side, taking care not to alter the relative position of his feet or his grip on the stick while doing so.

Methodical Series of drills: from the pushed pass with the player stationary and the ball at rest, to the pushed pass on the run with a moving ball.

1. Pushing the ball at rest paying attention to the hint already given.
2. Two players push the ball to each other. The player receiving the ball indicates to his partner by his position where he would like the ball to be passed.
3. Practising accurate pushes in pairs. The players must attempt to push the ball within the confines of a narrow lane or along the sideline itself.
4. Passing competition: two pairs of players stand opposite each other behind two lines marked out ten to twelve yards apart. In the middle between them, two posts are placed upright three or four feet apart. In a set period of time the players attempt to push the ball through the posts as many times as possible from their own position. The pair scoring the most goals within the prescribed time is the winner. As a variation, each player can also play his partner in order to decide the contest. Who will be the first to score ten goals? The winners can have another round, while the losers for their part can discover a consolation prize winner.
5. Pushing relay practice: There are four players in each team. The two halves of each team stand ten yards apart. Each player must make a pushed pass (from the side-on position) and then run after the ball and join the line-up opposite. Which team produces twenty pushed passes first or which team produces the most pushes in two minutes?
6. The ball is placed to the right of the back foot just in front of the body. After moving the ball about eighteen inches to the left to bring it midway between the feet, the ball, still rolling slowly, is pushed to one's partner.

7. The ball is moved to the left from the side-on position past the left (or front) foot along the intended line of the pass, overtaken my means of a chainstep (as if jumping out to drive in cricket)-left-right-left and then pushed to one's partner at the moment the left foot comes down for the second time and the left shoulder is pointing at the partner.

8. To learn the push while running at full speed, the ball has to be moved four or six yards away by the player himself. The player runs quickly after the ball, then, immediately before the push, he swings round from the frontal position to get into the necessary side-on position to the ball and pushers it to his partner, when the left foot comes to the front again.

9. Relay Practice: The first player dribbles the ball from the centre line to the twenty-five yards line. After running round a flag there, he pushes the ball, from there, back to the next player, who is waiting beyond the centre line. If the push is so weak that it fails to reach the line of players, the original player must run after it and push it a second time. On no account must the player waiting to receive the ball go into the area between the centre line and the twenty-five yards line, before the ball has crossed the line.

10. Who can push the ball, which is placed three paces away, furthest?

11. 'Chase the Ball': Practise chasing the ball across the width of the field between the centre line and the twenty-five yards line with two teams of three.

Wherever the ball is stopped, a pushed pass must be made towards the opponent's end of the playing area. The point of the game is to push the ball over the far line (the side line). If the ball goes over either of the 'touch lines' (the centre for twenty-five yards line), then it must be pushed back into play by 'the opposite side at the point at which it went over the line.

The winning side is either the one scoring the most points in a set period to time or the one scoring a set number of points first.

12. Pushing as in 7 to 10 above: But this time the right foot should be brought forward at the moment of impact.
13. Pushing on the run, to both left and right; this practice is done to a partner running level and parallel 10-15 yards away.

Free hits

When the ball goes over the goal-line of the defender sent by the opposite player, the last Back or one of the Backs takes a free-hit at the spot not beyond 16 yards opposite to the point from where the ball has gone out.

The free-hit taker must not make any mistake while taking the hit because it may prove fatal for his side. The free-hit may also be taken by giving a pass to another Full-Back positioned quite close to him provided there is no likely-hood of any interruption by the rival player. He should immediately take the hit if his forwards are free to receive it and the opposing players are not ready to block it. The forwards, specially nearest winger, must position himself at a convenient place where he can receive the ball safely.

Otherwise, the free hit should only be taken when the opposing forwards are properly marked, specially when the players of that direction, tend to take a hit.

The attacking forwards should always be quick in taking the proper position in order to regain the possession of the ball. Whereas the defending team's forwards should take position at a such place where the ball can reach safely.

The free-hit takers must practise hitting the dead ball without raising it.

A 16 yards hit is taken directly towards the left-winger and also through the gap. The hit taken towards the right-winger shown with an unbroken line is not correct as it is likely to be interrupted by the opposing side.

To avoid interruption it is safer to hit indirectly, as shown here, towards the player though unmarked but at a far distance.

All the free-hits upto the opponents 25 yards area should be taken by the wing backs and those within the 25 yard area may be taken by the half-backs except in the area covered by the circle where wing forwards are responsible to take free-hits as shown in the diagram. The right-winger takes the hit straight into the circle. The 16 yards hit immediately taken by giving a pass to another closer defender who safely sends the ball to his left-winger. A leading forward is still at the wrong position as he fails to take a proper position to block the free-hit.

Clearance within 16 yards area

The clearance shown by the dotted arrows are wrong,

since they diagonally across the striking circle. Players should be very careful in taking the bit while aiming to send the ball out of their danger zone i.e. within their own 16 yards area. Hits shown in broken lines are more advantageous to the opposing team if they are intercepted.

The goal-keeper and players aiming to make good clearance without creating any further danger for their team must make their hits in the direction shown with the unbroken lines.

Full-backs

The first and, perhaps the foremost quality, required of a first class back is coolness. Unless he can keep a clear head at the critical moment he will bring disaster to his side. Besides this, backs must possess good speed, a quick recovery when beaten and be able to hit the ball quickly, cleanly and powerfully. They must have tackling ability, very keen anticipation and a sense of positioning and, perhaps above all, perfect understanding between themselves to cover each other.

Fielding. A correct technique in fielding the ball is very important. A already discussed in an earlier chapter, the safest method to stop the ball, particularly when an attacking forward is approaching is to place your stick and body in the line of the ball. While doing so a full back may be running the risk of committing "kicks", but it is safer to take such a risk than allow the approaching forward to run away with the ball.

Hitting. Backs must be able to hit the ball hard without committing "sticks" to relieve pressure on their side. Hitting into an oncoming forward's legs is bad hockey and should be avoided. It is most important to remember that backs should not clear the ball from their 25 yard area towards the centre of the field and across the striking circle. Clearances must be made, as quickly as possible, straight ahead in the direction of the wing.

It is often observed that a full back in trying to clear from an awkward position either commits "sticks" or tries to dribble to bring himself into an easier position to effect the clearance, thus taking a very big risk of losing the ball at a critical moment. To get out of such difficulties it is easier and safer to pass the ball quickly to the nearest colleague for the clearance. It is a folly on the part of a full back to take a hard hit ranging the far away unmarked forward and ignoring one of his colleagues positioning in between.

Both backs should have a good mastery over stick-work to beat an opponent before clearing the ball but they should avoid dribbling as far as possible as this practice can prove very costly. They should avoid wild hitting. Good backs seldom attempt to hit the ball on the run. They should look out for the forward best placed to receive the ball and not hit it indiscriminately up the field.

Tackling. While tackling or intercepting short passes of the opposing forwards, a back cannot be successful unless he is a master of the art of transferring his stick from his right to his left very quickly. It is always better to tackle the forward before he has obtained complete possession of the ball.

The best method of tackling an opposing forward, in possession of the ball, is to advance patiently, instead of rushing wildly, with stick down and watching the ball very closely. It is better and safer to push the ball to the side lines than to bring the ball first into control from a difficult angle or from an awkward position and then to clear. Develop the art of quickness in clearing, removing the ball from a player in possession, interception, covering and correct timing in tackling, which are the essential attributes for a first class back. As a rule never dribble unless you are forced to do so. Finally, keep in mind that, however good you may be in tackling or intercepting these skills cannot fully utilized unless your clearances are accurate and quick.

Positioning. It is the duty of the left back to mark the opposing inside right, while the right back is responsible for the inside left. Sometimes the back is also required to tackle other opposing forwards and if such a situation arises he should not shirk doing so. The full backs must have a good understanding with their colleagues the half back and the goalkeeper. Most important is the ability to cover a colleague. Play diagonally. This method will not only spoil many good movements of the opposing forwards by putting them "off-side" but also place you in the best position to tackle before they get possession of the ball.

Generally speaking, the backs should at the commencement of the game be at the places shown in diagram 28 and as he attack progress, gradually advance and keep in close touch with the halves. Supposing the inside right is attacking near the 25-yard line, the position of the right back is roughly at the 50-yard line and the left back much deeper, say about the 25-yard line, covering the centre of the field. In this way any long through passes or hard drives would be easily dealt with by the rear back. The right back is in an advantageous position and is ready for any counter-attack and also he is in a position to tackle or intercept a pass to the opposing left wing. When the ball is approaching the 25-yard ling the back should closely mark his inside forward. The main thing to remember is that the oblique form must always be maintained, otherwise one forward through pass would defeat both backs with one stroke.

The backs are the last line of defence before the goal so their position in the hockey field is vital. More than any other player on the field they must be safe. I have seen many backs fumble or miss the ball. This is because they do not keep their eye on the ball but on the oncoming opponent. The backs should be able to stop the ball cleanly and accurately. The back should hit the ball hard. But this does not mean that they should hit anywhere just to clear the ball. They should hit towards their forwards so that they can make a move. There is a time when a left back must make a risky but an effective movement by hitting the ball across to his right-in. This may prove an effective move and might result in a goal.

In recent hockey we have seen many backs use obstructive methods to stop their opponent. This is contrary to the game of hockey. A good back is judged by his neat tackling. The full-back should adjust themselves with the half-backs to make a formidable defence. There should be a very good understanding with the wing half and when the wing half is beaten, the back should tackle the winger while the half comes back to cover the inside forward. The full backs should not stick to the rule of covering to tackling an opponent inside forwards only. There are times when they have to tackle an opponent other than the opposing inside. They should not let any member of the opposition take shot at the goal. The full backs should not rush on the forward tackle. They should not commit themselves. They should make the forward take the initiative and wait for him to make the mistake. Pretend to tackle and draw back again. If the full backs are sure of trapping the ball through the gap they should leave an apparent gap for the opponent to push the ball through and thus force him to part with the ball.

There should be a very good understanding between the two backs. The two backs should always avoid being parallel to each other. If the backs do this the defence is wide open. The back should always be one up, one down. If the backs playing up misses the ball, his partner moves across to take it. It is essential for the back to run fast while covering his partner. The back should never allow the rival forwards to catch them standing square.

The full backs should practice the technique of taking penalty corners. They should not only hit the ball hard but hit accurately in the corner of the net. Without practising you cannot master penalty corner hits. The best way of practising these is to keep a stump on the goal line 10 inches away from the corner post and try to hit the ball between the post and the stump. After a few months the backs should be able to hit about 90% of shots with great accuracy.

9

RULES AND REGULATIONS

Players entering the field before the players being substituted have left the field should be penalised in accordance. The duration of the game shall be two periods of thirty-five minutes each, unless otherwise agreed before the game. At half-time the teams shall change ends, and the duration of the interval shall not exceed five minutes, unless otherwise agreed before the game, but in no case shall it exceed ten minutes. The game starts when the umpire blows his whistle for the opening passback.

Guidance for Players and Umpires

(a) and (b) players and nominated substitutes, whether on or off the field of play, including any period of temporary or permanent suspension, are under the jurisdiction of the umpires during the whole match and are therefore subject to their decisions under the Rules of Hockey.

(i) Any player substituting for a goalkeeper is required to wear protective headgear. It is strongly recommended that a substitute for a goalkeeper wears appropriate protective clothing at all times.

(ii) All players involved in the substitution

procedure must be chosen from the players whose names appear on the approved team sheet, when required under competition regulations.

(iii) A player who has been substituted may reenter the field as a substitute for another player.

(iv) A suspended player may not be substituted whilst under suspension.

(v) Substitution of players may not take place following the award of a penalty corner or penalty stroke, except for the replacement of an incapacitated player.

(iv) Players leaving or entering the field shall do so at the centre line on the side of the field agreed with the umpires before the match, except in the cases of the substitution of a goalkeeper, when it shall be made within the circle, or the replacement of an incapacitated player who may not be able to leave at the centre line.

(vii) Substitution of a player may only be made after a player from the same team has left the field of play.

(viii) Captains are responsible for the operation of the substitute procedure during a game, unless otherwise agreed or there is a designated official.

(ix) Time shall not be stopped while substitutions are made other than for incapacitated players.

Each team must have a captain on the field who may wear a distinctive armband and who shall:

(a) toss for choice of start. The winner of the toss shall have

(i) the right to choose which end his team will attack in the first half

(ii) the right to have possession of the ball at the start of the game.

The winner of the toss having mad his choice, the opposing side will automatically have the second option. The team not having started the game will have possession of the ball for restarting after half-time.

(b) before the start of play and on any change, indicate, if necessary, to each other and to the umpires, their respective goalkeepers subject to Rules.

(c) in case he is substituted or suspended indicate to the umpires the player on the field who will replace him as captain.

(d) be responsible for the control procedure for the substitution of players, unless delegated to a designated or team official. When the procedure is conducted by a designated or team official the team captain is absolved of responsibility.

(e) be responsible for the behaviour of all his team players, except where the substitute players are under the control of a designated team official.

A breach of Parts (c), (d) or (e) of this Rule shall b penalised in accordance with Rule.

Umpires and Timekeepers

(a) There shall be two umpires to control the game and to administer the Rules.

These umpires shall be the sole judges of fair and unfair play during the game.

(b) Unless otherwise provided, each team shall be responsible for providing one umpire.

(c) Each umpire shall be:

   (i) primarily responsible for the decisions in his own half of the field, for the whole of the game without changing ends.

   (ii) solely responsible for decisions on the hit-in for the full length of his nearer side-line and his back line.

   (iii) solely responsible for decisions on 16-yard hits, corners, penalty corners, penalty strokes and goals in his own half and free hits in his own circle.

(d) The umpires shall be responsible for keeping time for the duration of the game. It shall be permissible to have a timekeeper or timekeepers. Such timekeepers shall take over those duties of the umpires which concern the keeping of time, the indication of the end of each half and the duration of the interval.

(e) Umpires shall allow the full or agreed time and shall keep a written record of the goals as they are scored.

(f) Time shall be stopped during enforced stoppages so that each half of actual play shall comply with Rule(e).

(g) Umpires and timekeepers shall be debarred from coaching during a game and during the interval.

(g) Umpires and timekeepers shall be debarred from coaching during a game and during the interval.

(h) Umpires shall only blow the whistle to:

(i) Start and end each half of the game.

(ii) enforce a penalty.

(iii) start and end a penalty stroke.

(iv) indicate, when necessary, that the ball has passed wholly outside the field of play.

(v) signal a goal.

(vi) re-start the game after a goal has been scored.

(vii) restart the game after a penalty stroke in which a goal was not scored or awarded.

(viii) suspend the game for any reason and re-start after such a suspension.

Umpires shall satisfy themselves before the game that, as far as is practicable, Rules 4 to 9 inclusive are observed. Umpires shall refrain from enforcing a penalty in cases where they are satisfied that by enforcing it an advantage would be given to the offending team. If the umpire primarily responsible appears to be over-running the time, then his colleague should stop play and consult him on the matter. The umpires should when necessary agree the amount of time to be added after each penalty stroke and after any substantial stoppage for accident or otherwise.

Field of play

(a) All lines used in the measurements of the field are to be 3 inches wide. The side-lines and back-lines including the goal-lines are part of the field of play.

(b) The field shall be rectangular, 100 yards long and

60 yards wide. Its boundaries shall be clearly marked out with lines in accordance with the Plan. The longer lines shall be called the side-lines and the shorter the back-lines including that part of the back-line between the goal posts called the goal-line

(c) The Centre-line and 25-yards lines shall be marked throughout their length.

(d) To assist in the control of the hit-in, across the centre line and each 25-yards line, parallel to and 5 yards from the outer edge of the side-lines a mark of 2 yards in length shall be made.

(e) A mark 12 inches in length shall be placed inside the field of play on each side-line and parallel to the back-line and 16 yards from its inner edge.

(f) For penalty corner hits, the field shall be marked inside the field of play on the back-lines on both sides of the goal at 5 yards and 10 yards from the other edge of the nearer goal-post such distance being to the further edge of those lines. For corner hits the field shall be marked inside the field of play on the back-line 5 yards from the outer edge of the side-line. All these marks to be 12 inches in length.

(g) A spot 6 inches in diameter shall be marked in front of the centre of each goal; the centre of the spot shall be 7 yards from the inner edge of the goal-line.

(h) No marks other than those shown on the plan are permissible on the playing surface.

(i) Flagposts of not more than 5 ft. nor less than 4 ft. in

height, shall be placed for the whole game at each corner of the field, and at the 25 yard line; those at the 25 yard line shall be 1 yard outside the side-lines as indicated on the plan.

Goals, posts etc.

(a) There shall be a goal at the centre of each back-line, consisting of two vertical posts 4 yards apart, joined together by a horizontal cross-bar 7 feet from the ground (inside measurements). The front base of the goal-post shall touch the outer edge of the back-line. The goal posts shall not extend upwards beyond the cross-bar, nor shall the cross-bar extend sideways beyond the goal-posts.

(b) The goal-posts and cross-bar shall be rectangular and shall be 2 inches wide not more than 3" nor less than 2" deep and shall be painted white.

(c) Nets shall be attached firmly to the goal-posts and the cross-bar, at intervals of not more than 6 inches, and shall be attached firmly outside the back-board and side-boards.

(d) A back-board, 18 inches in height and 4 yards in length, shall be placed at the foot of and inside the goal-nets. Side-boards 18 inches in height and a minimum 4 feet in length shall be placed at right angles to the back-lines. The side-boards shall be fixed to the back of the goal-posts, so that the width of the goal-posts is not effectively increased.

(e) No chocks shall be placed inside the goal to support any of the boards.

Umpires should check:

(i) that goal-posts are firmly fixed.

(ii) that the goal-posts and cross-bars painted white.

(iii) that the goal-posts are correctly placed in relation to the back-line.

(iv) that there are no holes or bad tears in the netting, that the goal-nets are properly attached and that goal-boards are inside the net and do not project beyond the back of the goal-posts.

Without such careful inspection there may be difficulty and even inaccuracy in making decisions of a critical nature. It is recommended that the back-board/ side-boards be painted in a dark colour.

Shooting Circles

In front of each goal a line shall be drawn 4 yards long, parallel to and 16 yards from the back-line. The 16 yards shall be measured from the inside front corner of the goal-posts to the outer edge of that line. This line shall be continued each way to meet the back-lines by quarter circles having the inside front corner of the goal-posts as centres. The space enclosed by these lines, including the lines themselves, shall be called the shooting circle (hereinafter referred to as "the circle".

The ball

(a) The ball shall be spherical with the specifications mentioned in this Rule.

(b) The weight of the ball shall not be more than 5¾ ounces (163 grammes), nor less than 5½ ounces (156 grammes).

(c) The circumference of the ball shall not be more than 9¼ inches (23.5 centimetres) nor less than 813/ 16 inches (22.4 centimetres).

(d) (i) The ball shall be hard: it may be solid or hollow, provided it meets the other specifications in this Rule. (ii) The ball shall have an outer surface of any natural or artificial material. The surface shall be smooth, but a seam or indentations are permitted provided they do not alter the shape of the ball. (iii) The inner portion of a solid ball may consist of any natural or artificial material in any composition or mixture, as long as it meets the other specifications in this Rule.

(e) The traditional colour of the ball is white, but the team captains may agree upon the use of a ball of any other colour, as long as it contrasts with the colour of the field of play.

(f) Umpires shall not permit the use of a ball that does in their opinion not comply with this Rule. Should a ball during a game deteriorate in such a way that it not longer meets the specifications of this Rule, it shall be replaced immediately. If the game has not been stopped for any reason and the ball is in Play when it becomes unusable, the game shall be stopped and restarted using a new ball in accordance with Rule 10(b).

Guidance for Players and Umpires

A ball to be used in international matches must also meet the detailed standards as laid down by the F.I.H. These will cover the hardness, balance, smoothness, surface, moisture absorbance, friction and bounce of the ball. These conditions may vary for different playing surfaces.

National Associations and clubs may, for their own competitions, tournaments and matches, set their own standards, but the specifications of this Rule must be met.

The Stick

(a) The stick shall have a flat face on its left-hand side only. The face of the stick is the whole of the flat side and that part of the handle for the whole of the length which is above the flat side.

(b) The head of the stick (i.e. the part below the lower end of the splice or join) shall be curved and shall be of wood and shall not be edged with or have any insets or fittings of metal or any other substance, nor shall there be any sharp edges or dangerous splinters. The maximum length of the curved head of the sticks, as measured from the lowest part of the flat face, shall not exceed 4 inches it shall not be cut square or pointed, but shall have rounded edges.

(c) The total weight of the stick shall not exceed 28 ounces, nor be less than 12 ounces and it shall be of such a size, inclusive of any covering, that it can be passed through a ring having as interior diameter of 5.10 centimetres.

(d) Umpires shall forbid the use of any stick which in their opinion does not comply with this Rule.

For any breach of this Rule any player concerned shall not be allowed on the field of play until such time as he has complied with this Rule. The Board has become increasingly aware of the variety of new "shapes" that are appearing in the handle of the hockey stick. As the Rules only require a stick to pass through a stick ring having an interior diameter of 5.10 cms and to weigh between 12 ounces and 28 ounces the Board has felt necessary to issue guidance upon what is acceptable. The handle of the stick has had a traditional shape and it is intended that this should be retained. However, it cannot be accurately described as straight because it is recognized that most handles are wider nearer the head than at the top of the handle.

Therefore, it has been agreed in principle that a stick with a deviation of up 2cms from either edge of the face of the handle shall be acceptable while providing this guidance, the Board wishes to make it clear that it has not given approval for any particular design, only an indication of the areas of tolerance which should be accepted. The Board also confirms that there is no intention to ban sticks which have been on the market for some years, but it will ban the introduction of new, more extreme ideas and shapes. Discussions are currently being held with all interested parties to agree a revised stick definition.

Players' Dress and equipment

(a) Each player shall wear the dress approved by his Association or Club, unless varied to avoid confusion in a particular game. Goal-keepers shall wear a colour different from that of their own team and that of their opponents. Players shall not have dangerous spikes, studs or protruding nails in footwear, or wear anything that may be dangerous to other players.

(b) The following protective equipment is permitted for use by goal-keepers only: Body Protectors, Pads, Kickers, Gauntlet Gloves Protective Headgear and Elbow Pads.

For any breach of this Rule any player concerned

shall not be allowed on the field of play until such time as he has complied with this Rule.

Goalkeepers are required to wear their shirt or other garments over any body protectors. Field players are strongly recommended to wear shin and ankle guards. Goalkeepers must wear protective headgear at all times except as provided. It is strongly recommended that other protective equipment be worn at all times.

To start or re-start the game

(a) To start the game, re-start it after half-time and after each goal scored, a "pass-back" shall be played at the centre of the field. The pass-back for the start of the game shall be made by a player of the team which did not make a choice of ends, after half-time by a player of the opposing team and after a goal has been scored, by a player of the team against whom the goal has been awarded. The pass-back, which may be pushed or hit, must not be directed over the centre line.

At the moment when the pass-back is taken, no player of the opposing team shall be within 5 yards of the ball and all players of both teams other than the player making the pass-back must be in their own half of the field. If the striker hit at but miss the ball, the pass-back still has to be taken. After taking the pass-back, the striker shall not play the ball again nor remain or approach within playing distance until it has been touched or played by an other player of either team.

Any delay which amounts to time wasting shall not be permitted.

The ball shall be placed on the ground between the two players. Each player shall tap with his stick, first the ground between the ball and his own back-line, and then, with the flat face of his stick, his opponent" stick, over the ball, three times alternately, after which one of these two players shall play the ball with his stick to put it into play. Until the ball is in play, all other players shall not stand within 5 yards of the ball. A bully shall not be played within 16 yards of the back-line or goal-line.

For a breach of Rule a free hit shall be awarded to the opposing team.

For a breach of Rule (ii) or (b)(iii) the bully shall be played again.

For persistent breaches of Rule 10(b)(ii) and (b)(iii) the umpire may award a free hit to the opposing team; or, for such breaches in the circle by a defender, a penalty corner.

Guidance for players and umpires

To start or re-start the game.

(a) At the "Pass Back" the ball shall not be raised intentionally. The player taking the "Pass Back" shall not be penalised if the ball lifts off the ground as long as the intention to play along the ground is clear.

(b) (ii) Much obstruction will be prevented if the two players are made to stand square, not moving their feet until the ball is in play. (iii) There is no requirement for players to be nearer their own back-line or goal-line than the ball is.

Scoring a Goal

(a) A goal is scored when the whole ball, having been hit or deflected by the stick of an attacker whilst in the circle and not having gone outside the circle, passes completely over the goal-line between the goal-posts and under the cross-bar- except in circumstances detailed in Rule, when a goal may not be awarded, and in circumstances detailed in Rule penalty 1, when a goal may be awarded. It is immaterial if the ball subsequently touch or be played by one or more defenders. If, during the game, the goal-posts and/or cross-bar become displaced, and the ball pass completely over the goal-line at a point which, in the umpire's opinion, be between where the goal-posts and/or under where the cross-bar, respectively should have been, a goal shall be awarded. The team scoring the greater number of goals shall be the winner.

Guidance for Players and Umpires

Scoring a Goal

The ball must be inside the circle when played by an attacker (although he himself may be outside). If it is played within the circle and then touches the stick or person of a defender or defenders before crossing the goal-line, a goal is scored.

Should the ball be played from outside the circle by an attacker and be diverted between the posts by a defender who is in or outside the circle within the 25 yard area, a corner should be given.

Conduct of play

I A player shall not:

(a) play the ball with the rounded side of the stick.

(b) take part in or interfere with the game unless he has his own stick in his hand.

"Own Stick" means the stick with which the player began to play, or any stick that he legitimately substitutes for it.

(c) Lift the stick over the head of or raise the stick in a manner that is dangerous, intimidating or hampering to another player when approaching, attempting to play, playing or stopping the ball, A ball above the height of a player's shoulder shall not be played or played at by any part of the stick.

(d) stop the ball with his hand or catch it.

(There is nothing in this rule which prevents a player using his hand to protect himself from a dangerously raised ball.)

(e) play the ball wildly, or play or kick the ball in such a way as to be dangerous in itself, or likely to lead to dangerous play, nor play the ball intentionally into any part of an opponent's body, including the feet and legs.

(f) deliberately stop, propel or deflect the ball on the ground or in the air with any part of the body TO HIS OR HIS TEAM ADVANTAGE.

(g) deliberately raise the ball from a HIT, except for a shot at goal.

(h) deliberately raise tea ball so that it will fall into the circle.

(i) use the foot or leg to support the stick in order to resist an opponent

(j) kick, pick up, throw, carry or propel the ball in any manner or direction except with the stick.

(k) hit, hook, hold, strike at or interfere with another player" stick.

(I) charge, kick, shove, trip, strike at or personally handle another player or player" clothing.

(m)obstruct by running between an opponent and the ball nor interpose himself or his stick as an obstruction.

A player may:

(a) play the ball only with the flat side of his stick which includes that part of the handle above the flat side.

(b) tackle from the left of an opponent provided that he play the ball without previous interference with the stick or person of his opponent.

(c) If he is a goalkeeper and the ball is inside his circle be allowed-contrary to the provisions of Rule nd (j)- to kick the ball, stop it with any part of his body, play, but not propel it with his hand and stop it with his stick above his shoulder, unless dangerous. No penalty shall be incurred if when stopping a shot at goal, the ball rebound off any part of the goalkeeper's body or his stick.

(a) if the ball become lodged in one of the pads of a goalkeeper or in the clothing of any player or umpire the umpire shall stop the game and re-start it by a bully on the spot to be chosen by the umpire in whose half of the ground the incident occurred

(b) If the ball strikes an umpire or any loose object on the pitch, including any piece of playing equipment dropped accidentally, the game shall continue. Any deliberate action by a player in throwing his stick or other piece of playing equipment on to the pitch, at the ball, at an opponent or at an umpire, should be penalised

Misconduct

Rough or dangerous play, any delay which amounts to time wasting, deliberate breaches of any rule, or any other behaviour which in the umpire's opinion amounts to misconduct, shall not be permitted.

Penalties

Outside the circle.

- A free hit shall be awarded to the opposing team. An umpire shall award a penalty corner for an offence by any defender in his own 25 yards area, when, in the umpire" opinion, the offence was deliberate.
- Inside the circle-by an attacker.
- A free hit shall be awarded to the defending team.
- Inside the circle-by a defender.

For a breach inside the circle by a defender a penalty corner shall be awarded or a penalty stroke if, in the umpire" opinion.

- Inside and outside the circle.

For a simultaneous breach of this Rule by two opponents, the umpire shall order a bully to be played on the spot where the breach occurred

- Inside and outside the circle.

For rough or dangerous play or misconduct, in addition to awarding the appropriate penalty, the umpire may:

(i) warn the offending player(s) which may also be indicated by showing a green card.

(ii) suspend him temporarily for not less than five minutes which may also be indicated by showing a yellow card.

A temporarily suspended player shall remain behind his own goal or in such other places as designated before the game, until allowed by the umpire by whom he was suspended to resume play or to be substituted: when necessary changing ends at the start of the second half of the game.

The penalties for rough and dangerous play, misconduct, deliberate breaches of the Rules, or time-wasting, should be noted carefully, and the appropriate penalty awarded. Persistent breaches of the Rules may suitably be dealt with under this Rule. If rough or dangerous play becomes prevalent, a word of caution to the offender(s) should effectively prevent the game getting out of hand. For those breaches of the Rule inside the circle Rule should also be taken into consideration.

Nothing in these Rules prevents a temporarily suspended player joining his team during the half-time interval but he should return to the suspended player's position on resumption of the second half of play unless his suspension has been ended.

Off-Side

At the moment when the ball is played a player of the same team as the pusher or striker is in an offside position if he be in his opponents' 25 yards area unless he be behind the ball or there be at least two opponents nearer to their own back-line or goal-line than he is.

For the purpose of this Rule, a player of either team shall be deemed to be on the field of play even though he be outside the side-line or behind the back-line or goal-line. A player who is in an off-side position shall not play or attempt to play the ball or gain any advantage for his team or influence the play of an opponent.

Guidance for players and umpires

The question of whether a player if off-side is governed by where he was at the moment when the ball was played by a player of the same team not where he is when he received the ball. The umpire must always have this in mind otherwise he may easily give a wrong decision. The act of "playing" the ball includes when a player of the same team is dribbling the ball. A player in a off-side position whether on or off the field should not be penalised unless he influence the play of an opponent or gain some advantage from his off-side position.

A player who is level with the ball is off-side.

A player cannot be off-side if:

he is nearer the 25 yards line than the ball is at the time it is played by a player of the same team. There are at least two opponents nearer to their own back-line than he is at the moment when the ball is played by a player of the same team.

If a player is off-side, he is not automatically put on-side by returning to his own side of his opponents 25 yards line to play the ball.

A whole line of forwards having outdistanced the defence and only having the goalkeeper in front of them could pass and repass to each other without being off-side as long as they keep behind the ball.

A player who is left off-side after making a previous shot should no to be penalised if he is trying to get back on-side, unless he is obstructing or distracting any opponent.

Free hit

(a) A free hit shall be taken on the spot where the breach occurred except that:

(i) for a breach by an attacker within the circle it shall be taken either from any spot within that circle

Or from any spot within 16 yards of the inner edge of the defending team's back-line or goal-line on a line drawn through the place where the breach occurred and parallel to the side-line.

(ii) for a breach by an attacker outside the circle but within 16 yards of the defending teams's back-line it shall be taken from any spot within 16 yards of the inner edge of the defending team's back-line on a line drawn through the place where the breach occurred and parallel to the sideline.

(b) The ball shall be stationary and the striker shall push or hit it. The ball must be moved and shall not be raised internationally or in such a way as to be dangerous in itself, or likely to lead to dangerous play.

(c) At the moment when the free hit is taken, no player of the opposing team shall remain within 5 yards of the ball. However, for a free hit to the attacking team within 5 yards of the circle, players of both teams, except the striker, shall be at least 5 yards from the ball. Should the umpire consider that a player is standing within 5 yards of the ball in order to gain time, the free hit shall not be delayed.

(d) If the striker hit at but miss the ball, provided that Rule has not been contravened, the free hit still has to be taken.

(e) After taking the free hit, the striker shall not play the ball again nor remain or approach within playing distance until it has been touched or played by an other player of either team.

Penalties

1. Inside the circle.

A penalty corner or penalty stroke shall be awarded to the attacking team.

2. Outside the circle.

A free hit shall be awarded to the opposing team An umpire shall award a penalty corner for a offence by any defender in his own 25 yards area, when in the umpire's opinion, the offence was deliberate.

Free Hit

The free hit must be taken from the right place and the ball must be stationary. If a player taking a free hit gains extra advantage by taking the free hit from the wrong place, h should be penalised. A free hit in the circle may be taken from any place within the circle.

Should there be any unnecessary delay by the players of the offending side in observing the 5-yards distance Rule, the umpire need not order the hit to be taken again but should warn offending players. The application of Rule, Penalty should be considered if an opponent knocks the ball away after a free hit has been awarded. At the free hit, the ball shall not be raised intentionally. The player taking the free hit shall not be penalised if the ball lifts off the ground as long as the intention to play along the ground is clear. Simply touching the ball with the stick is not considered to be a hit; the ball must from its original position.

Penalty Corner

(a) A penalty corner shall be awarded to the opposing team if, in the umpire's opinion: (i) there has been an *intentional* breach of Rules inside the 25 yards area but outside the circle by a player of the defending team (ii) an *unintentional* breach of Rule, inside the circle or an *intentional* breach of Rule inside the circle by a player of the defending team. (iii) for persistent breaches of Rule or (b) (iii) in the circle by a defender.

(b) A player of the attacking team shall push or hit the ball from a spot on the back-line not less than 10 yards from the goal-post, on whichever side of the goal the attacking team prefers. The player concerned is required to have at least one foot outside the field of play when taking the penalty corner.

The ball shall not be raised intentionally but the hit or push shall not be penalised if the ball lifts off the ground without causing danger or appearing likely to lead to dangerous play.

(c) At the moment when such push or hit is made, no other player shall be within 5 yards of the ball. The rest of the attacking team shall be in the field of play with both sticks and feet outside the circle not more than five of the defending team shall stand with both sticks and feet behind their own goal-line or back-line. The rest of the defending team shall be beyond the centre-line.

(d) Until the ball be pushed or hit not attacker shall ente the circle nor shall a defender cross the goal-line, back-line or centre-line.

(e) (i) No shot at goal shall be made from a penalty corner until the ball b stopped or come to rest on the ground or touch the stick or person of a defender. The defending goalkeeper shall remain on his feet until the first shot at goal has been made. (ii) If the first shot at goal is a *hit,* the ball shall not cross the goal-line at a height higher than the back-board/side-boards (18 inches) unless it has touched the stick or person of a defender. (iii) If the ball travels beyond 5 yards from the outer edge of the circle line, the penalty corner is ended and the special provisions mentioned in (i) and (ii) no longer apply.

(f) The player taking the penalty corner hit or push from the back line shall not, after striking the ball, play the ball again nor approach or remain within playing distance of the ball until it has been touched or played by another player of either team.

(g) If the striker of the penalty corner hit at or push at but miss the ball the penalty corner still has to be taken.

(h) No goal shall be scored directly by the player taking the penalty corner hit or push from the back-line, even if the ball be played into goal by a defender.

Penalties

1. Attacker(s) entering the circle or defender(s) crossing the goal-line, back-line or centre-line too soon or coming within 5 yards of the ball too soon- the penalty corner may, at the discretion of the umpire, be taken again.
2. For persistent breaches of Rule by the attackers— The umpire may award a free hit.
3. For persistent breaches of Rule by the defenders— The umpire may award a penalty stroke.
4. For an unintentional breach of Rule by the goalkeeper—The penalty corner may, at the discretion of the umpire, be taken again.
5. For intentional or persistent breaches of Rule by the goalkeeper-the umpire shall award a penalty stroke.
6. For any other breach of Rule A free hit shall be awarded to the defending team.

Under the mandatory experiment the ball must be put back into play from the backline within the circle and stopped outside the circle.

Both teams should be correctly positioned. There is nothing within this Rule which prevents attackers or defenders from leaning into the circle provided their bodies and sticks are not touching the ground within the circle. The umpire has the right to order the penalty corner to be taken again if an attacker crosses the circle line or if a defender crosses the goal-line, back-line or centre-line before the ball is played. This power should, however, be used with discretion if the breach is by a defender. It can be to the disadvantage of the attackers to stop the game when the hit-out has been well made, well stopped and resulted in an attacker being in a good position to shoot. As a Mandatory Experiment, the ball must be stopped outside the circle. The ball may be deflected or passed one or more times by the attacking players, but it must be stopped or come to a stop at some time outside with in 5 yards of the circle before a shot at goal is made. If the ball travels beyond 5 yards from the outer edge of the circle, there is no need for it to be stopped as the penalty corner has ended.

Although the first *hit* must not cross the goal-line above a height of 18 inches, there is no limit to the height of a push, flick or scoop or of any subsequent stroke, subject always to there being no danger. No is there any limit to the height of a *hit* before it crosses the line subject always to there being no danger.

At the moment when the penalty corner hit or push from the backline is taken, the goalkeeper may remain on the goal-line or move to another position but he is not allowed to lie down until the first shot at goal has been made. As soon as that first shot (be it a hit, push, flick, or scoop) has been made, the goalkeeper is permitted to dive, kneel, slide etc. in the usual manner. It is the act of deliberately grounding himself before the first shot, that is denied to the goalkeeper by Rule; consequently the goalkeeper shall not be penalised if he make an involuntary fall or if his act be induced by the actions of his opponents, in which case the umpire may order that the penalty corer be taken again. The goalkeeper may also give, slide, etc whenever he gets within playing distance of the ball before the first shot at goal has been made.

If the ball has not previously been touched by a defender, or has not been stopped on the ground, a flying hit following a pass or deflection from one attacker to another, should be penalised as a breach of this Rule.

"Directly" means before another player of the attacking team has played the ball. There is no requirement for a different attacking player to play the ball if it has been played by a defender as it is then in normal play.

For a breach of any Rule by the goalkeeper which prevents a goal from being scored, a goal shall be awarded to the opposing team. For a breach of any Rule by an attacker, the game shall be re-started with a free hit to be taken by a defender from a spot in front of the centre of the goal-line and 16 yards from the inner edge of that line. For a breach of clause (b)(iii) or (d)(i) the umpire may order the stroke to be taken again.

Note the cases in which this may be awarded, and that it shall be awarded if, in the umpire's opinion, an intentional breach of Rules has been committed inside the circle even though it may seem to the umpire improbable that, but for the breach, a goal could have been scored. The intentional breach must be against a player who either has possession of the ball or the opportunity to gain possession of the ball. It should be particularly noted that this penalty is intended to meet offences which may materially affect the game, when a more severe penalty than a penalty corner is necessary, and it should be applied accordingly by umpires.

It is not always easy for an umpire to decide whether a breach is intentional or not, but a distinction should be made between committing a breach of the Rules that is entirely forbidden, such as charging, and a breach which is the result of an attempt to do something lawful. A defender must show by his actions that he has tried to prevent fouling an attacker e.g. charging into a player about to shoot from a favourable position should invariably be regarded as intentional for the purpose of this Rule.

If a goalkeeper falls on or beside the ball in front of goal, an award of a penalty stroke would be appropriate in most cases where the opponents thereby have no fair view of the ball or opportunity to play the ball.

If there is any unreasonable delay or misconduct by either a defender or an attacker in carrying out any of the provisions of this Rule, the umpire may treat such action as misconduct and deal with it accordingly. For a breach of Rules a free hit from 16 yards from the centre of the goal shall be awarded.

Ball outside field of play

When the whole ball passes completely over the back-line and no goal is scored, or over the side-line, it is out of play and the game shall be re-started as in Rules.

Over-side line

(a) When the whole ball passes completely over the side-line, it or another ball, shall be placed on the line at the spot at which it crossed the side-line. The ball shall be pushed or hit without undue delay by a player of the team opposed to the player who last touched it in play. This player is not required to be wholly inside or outside the side-line when making his push or hit.

(b) The ball shall be stationary and the striker shall push or hit it. The ball must be moved and shall not be raised intentionally or in such a way as to be dangerous in itself or likely to lead to dangerous play.

(c) At the moment wen the push or hit is taken no player of the opposing team shall be within 5 yards of the ball. If any player of the opposing team be within 5 yards of the ball, the umpire may require the push or hit to be taken again. If however, in the umpire's opinion, a player of the opposing team remain within 5 yards of the ball to gain time, the push or hit shall not be delayed.

(d) If the striker hit at but miss the ball, provided that Rule has not been contravened, the push or hit still has to be taken.

(e) After taking a push or hit the player shall not play

the ball again, nor remain or approach within playing distance of the ball until it has been touched or played by another player of either team.

Penalty

For any branch of this Rule, a free hit shall be awarded to the opposing team.

(a) By an attacker or by a defender from more than 25 yards from his own back-line.

(i) When the ball passes completely over the back-line off one of the attacking team and no goal is scored, or off one of the defending team over his own back-line or goal-line who is more than 25 yards from the back-line, the game shall be restarted without undue delay by a push or hit taken by one of the defending team from a spot opposite the place where it crossed the back-line or goal-line and not more than 16 yards from the inner edge of that line.

(ii) The ball shall be stationary and the striker shall push or hit it. The ball must be moved and shall not be raised intentionally or in such a way as to be dangerous in itself or likely to lead to dangerous play.

(iii) No player of the opposing team shall be within 5 yards of the ball when the push or hit is taken.

(iv) If the striker hit at but miss the ball, provided that Rule has not been contravened, the push or hit still has to be taken.

(v) After taking the push or hit, the striker shall not play the ball again nor remain nor approach within playing distance of the ball until it has been touched or played by another player of either team.

(b) By a defender.

When the ball has been unintentionally hit by, or glanced off, the stick or person of a defender and has gone over his own back-line or goal line from within his own 25 yards area a push or hit shall be taken by the attacking team as follows, unless a goal has been scored.

(i) The player shall push or hit the ball from a spot on the back-line within 5 yards of the corner flag nearer to the point where the ball crossed the back-line.

(ii) The ball shall be stationary and the striker shall push or hit it. The ball must be moved and shall not be raised intentionally or in such a way as to be dangerous in itself or likely to lead to dangerous play.

(iii) No player of the opposing team shall be within 5 yards of the ball when the push or hit is taken.

(iv) If the striker hit at but miss the ball, provided that Rule has not been contravened, the push or hit still has to be taken.

(v) After taking the push or hit, the striker shall not play the ball again nor remain or approach within playing distance of the ball until it has been touched or played by another player of either team.

Penalties

For a breach of this Rule by an attacker, a free hit shall be awarded to the defending team. For a ball raised dangerously from a free hit within the circle by a defender, a penalty corner shall be awarded. For an unintentional breach of this Rule by a defender outside the circle a free hit seal be awarded to the attacking team.

For an unintentional breach of this Rule inside the circle or for an intentional breach of this Rule by a defender within the 25 yards area but outside the circle, a penalty corner shall be awarded. For an intentional breach of this Rule by a defender within the circle, a penalty stroke shall be awarded. No player may deliberately play or deflect the ball over his own back-line or goal-line from an area enclosed by the 25 yards line, including the circle.

Guidance for Players and Umpires

When pushed or hit, the ball shall not be raised intentionally. The player taking the push or hit shall not be penalised if the ball lifts off the ground as long as the intention to play along the ground is clear. Simply touching the ball with the stick is not considered to be a push or hit; the ball must move from its original position.

Accidents

If a player or an umpire be incapacitated, the umpire or other umpire shall stop the game temporarily. In either case, if a goal be scored before the game be stopped it shall be allowed if, in the umpire's opinion, it would have been scored had the accident not occurred.

The umpire shall re-start the game as soon as possible, by:

(i) a bully on a spot to be chosen by the umpire in whose half of the ground the accident occurred.

(ii) the appropriate penalty when the accident was the result of a breach of the rules.

(iii) the implementation of a decision given before the game was stopped.

If the umpire concerned cannot continue, the other umpire or a replacement or reserve umpire shall restart the game.

The umpire should see that an injured player leaves the field of play as soon as possible, unless medical reasons prohibit this action.

Code of signals for umpires

Bully	Make a "Bully" movement with both hands.
Kicks	Slightly raise a leg an touch it with the hand.
Advantage	Indicate by extending an arm in the direction in which the benefiting team is playing and moving the hand from the wrist in waving motion to indicate movement in the required direction.
Obstruction	Make a circular movement with one arm in front of the body.

Obstruction (third party)	Cross forearms in front of body.
Goal Scored	Turn, and point both arms horizontally towards the centre of the ground.
Off-side	Stand on the line of decision and point one arm horizontally along that line. Then as a separate signal indicate the direction of the free hit.
Hit-in from side-line	Indicate the direction with one arm raised horizontally; point downwards with the other arm.
Free Hit and Directional Signal	Indicate the direction with one arm raised Horizontally.
16-yards Hit	Extend both arms out sideways.
Hit-in from back-line	Point one arm at the corner flag nearer to the point where the ball crossed the back-line.
Penalty Corner	Point both arms horizontally towards the goal.
Penalty Stroke	With one arm point to the penalty spot, and the other arm point straight up in the air. This signal also indicates time stopped.
Dangerous Play	and/or bad Tempers. both hands horizontally, palms downwards, in front of the body, moving them slowly up and down. Indicate penalty if necessary.

Time Stopped	Turn towards the other umpire and/or time keeper(s) and cross fully extended arms at the wrists above the head.

Signals for kicks and obstruction may be shown if there is doubt about the reason for the decision.

Rules of Hockey

The Rules of Hockey leave much to the individual interpretation of the Umpire. By their very nature, such elements as dangerous play, the lifted ball bad obstruction will depend upon the relevant position of other players. Although the Rules Book includes Guidance for Players and Umpires, it is thought that the following require further explanation to try to ensure more consistent interpretation by Umpires.

Time wasting

A player may be considered to be wasting time if, having taken up a proper position with the ball and other players are in their correct positions, and unreasonable amount of time elapses before the ball is put into play. This also applies to the penalty stroke after the whistle has been blown to start the penalty.

Lifted Ball

The raised ball must be judged on its dangerous aspects at the spot from where the ball is played, during flight and where the ball lands. The breach of the Rules should be penalised on the spot where the danger occurs, not necessarily from where the ball was originally played.

(a) If the danger occurs at the place from where the ball has been played, the penalty must be taken from there.

(b) If the danger occurs at the place from where the ball lands, the penalty must be taken from there.

(c) When the danger occurs during the flight of the ball, the penalty should be taken from the place from which the ball originally came.

The only exception would be if a player of either team behaved in an unnecessarily dangerous manner in the area o the flight of the ball. Particular attention should be given to any flick or scoop made with an oncoming opponent within 5 yards. Danger is almost certain and should be penalised.

(d) When a ball is deliberately raised so that it falls directly into the circle a free hit should be awarded from the spot where the ball was raised.

It is important to realise that not every ball entering the circle off the ground is forbidden. A ball which bounces into the circle from a lofted stroke must b judged solely on its dangerous aspects. A hit entering the circle off the ground must also be judged according to the dangerous play rule.

(e) A ball raised over an opponent" stick or body whilst on the ground is permitted, subject as always to the raised ball not being dangerous or likely to lead to dangerous play.

Any player receiving a lifted ball must be given the opportunity to play it in a safe manner. If that player is clear of other players at the time ball is lifted, no players of the opposing side should approach within 5 yards of that player until the ball has been played and on the ground. Any player doing so should be penalised with a free hit. In the set-play situation of a corner hit from the back-line, a hit should be penalised as dangerous if it is raised into the circle into players.

Note that this does not mean that every corner hit which is not hit along the ground is to be penalised. The raised ball which is hit into the open, or to a player on his own, should not be penalised. Despite this, however, if a ball goes to a lone defender and (in the opinion of the umpire) deflects dangerously upwards from his stick because the original hit was raised off the ground, then the initial corner striker and not the defender is to be penalised.

Right of the Goalkeeper

If the goalkeeper propels the ball off or by any part of his body over the cross-bar or around a goal post, it is not a breach of Rule. Such propulsion is only allowed as a reaction to hits, pushes, scoops or flicks at goal. Propelling a stationary ball by hand is not allowed and must be penalised according to the penalties in Rule. The goalkeeper is permitted to stop the ball above his shoulder with his stick within his circle, provided that such action is not dangerous or likely to lead to dangerous play.

The practice of the goalkeeper lying down intentionally across the face of the goal before the first shot at goal at a penalty corner is prohibited. This interpretation relates only to the practice of the goalkeeper lying down intentionally across the face of the goal before the first shot, and does not prohibit a goalkeeper from making a sliding tackle or from diving to stop a shot at goal.

This interpretation should not be used to penalise

a goalkeeper who ends up lying on the ground, defending his goal following the First Shot at goal.

The following should be noted:

(a) If the goalkeeper is within striking distance of the ball, he can slide or dive.

(b) If the ball touches a defender or goes 5 yards outside the circle, the penalty corner is over and the goalkeeper may lie down.

(c) If the goalkeeper goes down as a result of a dummy shot, e.g. a lay-off, and then tries to get up again, There is no breach.

(d) If the goalkeeper goes down before the first shot at goals as a result of a dummy shot, and remains down internationally a penalty stroke is to be blown.

(e) After the first shot at goal, goalkeeper can defend their goals in any way they wish.

It is generally agreed that it is extremely difficult for umpires to determine whether the goalkeeper goes to ground before or after the first shot. So, the goalkeeper should be penalised only when the umpires are certain that a breach has occurred. It is more important for the game that the umpire ensures that the ball has been properly stopped by the attackers or touched by a defender before a shot is more than that this be missed while checking the position of the goalkeeper.

The practice of a goalkeeper lying down across the goal before the first shot at goal is to be treated as dangerous play and, in view of the instructions given, intentional. As such, the appropriate penalty for a goalkeeper who so lies down is:

First offence	Penalty stroke
Second offence	penalty stroke + Green card
Third offence	Penalty stroke + Yellow and then Red cards

Dangerous play can result from the actions of a player towards other players or to himself.

A goalkeeper is strongly recommended to wear protective clothing because it is considered that the role he has to play in the game has a potential for danger from the ball or even sticks. The wearing of such protective clothing does not permit him to behave unfairly towards other player-such actions as diving head first at opponents or kicking wildly either at the ball or opponent" stick should be penalised.

Suspension of Goalkeepers

Under the conditions of Rule "..each team shall have one goalkeeper on the field or shall indicate a field player who has the privileges of a goalkeeper" As a result, following the suspension of a goalkeeper, the Captain has to make a choice between:

(a) Replacing the suspended goalkeeper with another goalkeeper;

(b) Nominating a field player to put on protective headgear and such other protective clothing as considered necessary (time must be provided for this).

If option (a) is followed, the replacement goalkeeper can only enter the field as a substitute for a field player, thus ensuring that the team has only 10 players on the field of play. If option (b) is followed, the team will have only 10 players on the field. However, Hockey Regulations may require that protective headgear be worn at all times by the stand-in goalkeeper, who will be expected to act in a manner similar to that of a normal goalkeeper. This, while permitted to play the ball outside the circle with his stick, he will not be permitted to behave in a manner different from that of his fully-protected predecessor.

At the end of a temporary suspension, the Captain is faced with the following options:

(a) If the temporarily suspended goalkeeper returns to play as goalkeeper, then the replacement goalkeeper should remove the protective clothing and become a normal field player. Under the circumstances of (a) above, if the replacement goalkeeper is not required as a field player, a normal substitution needs to be made. If the previously-suspended goalkeeper is not required on the field of play and is replaced by a field player, the substitution should be made in the normal way.

(b) Under the circumstances of (b) above, the suspended goalkeeper returns and the "stand-in" goalkeeper returns to be a field player. However, the suspended goalkeeper could be properly substituted by another goalkeeper.

Suspension of Players

In addition to the awarding of various penalties for breaches of the Rule, Umpires are provided with powers to warn and/or suspend players when circumstances justify. The Rules are clear that such powers are an addition to existing penalties, not a substitution for them. It is important therefore that they should be used thoughtfully and have a clear purpose in mind.

Umpires must remember that if a card is used for an offence early in game, they have set the precedent for the remainder of that game. It is important to be consistent so think carefully before using the card. There are no rules about the sequence in which cards should be used. Their main purpose is to communicate decisions to the other umpire, players, technical officials and spectators. They may be given for various offences. However, there are some general principles governing their use. Under certain circumstances, and they will not be that common, a player could receive two green cards or even two yellow cards for different offences during the same game. Where an offence for which a card has been awarded is repeated, the same colour card should not again be used. When a second yellow card is awarded, albeit for a different offence from the first, it would be normal for the period of suspension to be longer than the original one, Once a yellow card has been shown to player, that player cannot receive a green card. Any offence involving violence should not be followed by a card of a similar colour, i.e. a yellow card for violence can only b followed by a red card. Umpires should keep a note of players to whom cards have been shown, together with the length of suspension where appropriate, and should exchange and confirm this information at half-time.

Interpretation of obstruction in Hockey has changed significantly over the last few years. The main reasons for this are the increased use of artificial pitches on which the ball and player can change direction quickly, a desire to let the game flow and a wish to develop and protect skills on the ball.

The stationary player

In the past, only the direction the receiving player was facing was considered rather than what the receiver and tackler where trying to do.

Now the principles are:

The receiving, stationary player may be facing in any direction.

The onus is on the tackler to move into position, i.e. usually to move round the receiver, to attempt a legitimate tackle.

Thus, the tackler must not crash into a receiver and thereby try to claim obstruction, any such action should be firmly penalised.

Having collected the ball, the receiver must move away in any direction (except, of course, bodily into the tackler).

Accordingly, the receiver is being allowed to collect the ball and proceed with play-with the onus on the tackler to move in position where an attempt can be made to play the ball without contact with the receiver.

The moving player

The variations in this instance are vast-so a few principles for making the necessary judgement are suggested.

One way of summarising these principles is to consider the position, intent and timing of the tackler. Just as with the stationary receiver, the onus is on the tackler to be in, and if necessary move to, a position from which a legitimate tackle can be made. Even once in the correct position, the following conditions must also be satisfied before obstruction occurs.

There must be an intention to make a tackle. In essence, the tackler must be attempting to move his stick towards the ball. The timing of this movement of stick towards ball must be precise-because until the moment the tackler is in a tackling position and intent on making the tackle, the player with the ball can move off with the ball in any direction.

This is the essence of the current interpretation of obstruction: allowing a player to receive a ball, play or pass it in any direction, and only penalising him if obstruction takes place at the time a properly-placed tackler is intent on making the tackle. That is, the player with the ball can play Hockey, and is penalised only if obstruction is actual rather than implied.

Play is interrupted many times during a match for obstruction. Some of those interruptions result from breaches which have been manufactured, which means that the opponents have been forced into breaching unintentionally one of the Rules.

Forcing an opponent into an obstructive position, often emphasised by running into the opponent or by waving his stick over his opponent, are actions which must be penalised. A player shall not play the ball intentionally into an opponent" foot, leg or body" If he does, then the umpire may decide to let play go or penalise the offence with a free hit or a penalty corer if it is done by a defender in his own circle.

There are a number of occasions when players will intentionally breach the Rules to gain an advantage for their team. Such occasions will include knocking the ball away after a free hit has been awarded, picking the ball up and carrying it away before returning it to the opposing team, playing the ball with the hand or above the shoulder with the stick. All intentional breaches must be penalised in accordance with the penalties set out in the rules. Strict action taken early in a game will usually result in non-repetition of the offence. However, if such action does not get the required results, penalty 5 (i) and (ii) should be activated. Only in exceptional circumstances should 5 (iii) be used.

(1) There are a number of occasions when players will intentionally breach he Rules to gain an advantage for their team. Such occasions will include:

Knocking the ball away after a free hit has been awarded.

Picking the ball up and carrying it away before returning it to the opposing team.

All intentional breaches must be penalised in accordance with the penalties set out in the Rules. Strict action taken early in a game will usually result in a non-repetition of the offence.

However, if such action does not get the required result, either a Green or a Yellow card is appropriate.

Umpires should be prepared to reverse their decisions in the face of dissent from players. This interpretation of the misconduct rule is most effective. Where a decision is reversed, umpires should blow the whistle again and indicate the new direction and the player causing the new decision to be made.

It has of course always been possible to increase the penalty, e.g. from an attacker's free hit inside the 25-yards line to a penalty corer, if the dissent is from the team defending a free it. But note that a penalty corner cannot be changed to a penalty stroke in this instance.

Offside

A player is no offside because of his positioning but because of his actions when in that position. Such actions must not gain an advantage for his team or influence the play of an opponent. The critical point is where that player was when the ball was last played by a member of the same team. A player dribbling the ball is playing the ball even though he might not pass it to another player. The position of a colleague can be of influence to defenders. A player cannot be played "on side" by the ball" being played or even touched by an opponent.

Free Hit

Requires that a Free Hit shall b taken on the spot where the breach occurred for exceptions) and the ball shall be stationary before the push or hit is taken.

Regarding the right spot, Umpires must be a little lenient, but when a team gains an extra advantage by breaching the above Rule, a free hit must be awarded to the opposing team. Regarding the ball being stationary, there should be no leniency even to the extent of awarding a penalty-corner for persistent breaches of the Rule within the circle or 25 yard area.

It should be noted that the free hit has been taken when the ball undergoes some movement after the push or hit has been taken. Placing the stick on a stationary ball is not an execution o the free hit. Umpires should remember that while players of the opposing team are required to be 5 yards from the ball when the push or hit is taken, they must be given sufficient time to do so before they are penalised. The free hit does not have to be delayed until they are, such action would be detrimental to the flow of the game. However, players of the opposing team who delay the taking of the free hit by whatever means not withdrawing 5 yards, hitting the ball away, handling the ball before returning it to the opposing team, should be penalised as appropriate, more severely for persistent breaches. Umpires should not penalise every free hit when the ball lifts slightly off the ground, so long as the intention to play along the ground is clear and the hit itself is not dangerous or leading to dangerous play.

Penalty corner

No shot at goal shall be made from a penalty corner until the ball be stopped or come to rest on the ground or touch the stick or person of a defender. The defending goal keeper shall remain on his feet until the first shot at goal has been made.

When stopped the ball must be stationary, although it may be spinning on the spot, which sometimes happens on artificial surfaces. There is no requirement that the ball must be stopped by the stick. It could just cease to move on its own.

A first hit at goal which is higher than the back-board or side-boards when the ball crosses the goal-line must be penalised even if the ball touches one of them as the result of a deflection downwards off the stick or body of a defender. The ball may be higher than the back-board or side-boards during its flight before it crosses the goal-line provided there is no danger.

The "First hit" is the first hit at goal after the ball has been stopped regardless of the number of times the ball has been passed or deflected, before or after the stop, provided it has not been played by or touched the stick or body of a defender. If it has been, the dangerous play rule will apply.

If at any time during a penalty corner the ball goes 5 yards or more beyond the edge of the circle, the ball is deemed to be in normal field play and therefore only subject to the dangerous play rule. Under these circumstances, there is no requirement for the ball to be stopped before a hit at goal can be made. The first hit at goal under all other circumstances must not cross the goal-line at a height higher than the top of the back-board or side-boards.

Every stroke following the first hit or other stroke remains subject to the Rules of dangerous play. High flicks or scoop strokes are permitted at any time subject to the Rule governing dangerous play.

As long as there are players in the circle in front of goal, every high shot may be dangerous. Special attention must be given to the breach by defenders of crossing the goal-line or back-line too early.

Some players put the ball back into play by using

a stroke different from the traditional hit or push. This stroke takes the form of a dragging action in which the ball is moved from a position behind the rear foot and does not leave the stick until it has passed the front foot. This is acceptable provided the ball is played with the flat face of the stick and only played once, i.e., it does not leave the head of the stick only to be touched again during the stroke by the same stick.

A penalty stroke should be awarded when a defender commits a breach of the Rules inside the circle against a player of the opposing team who has possession of the ball or is likely to gain possession of the ball.

The Rule requires that the push or hit may be taken up to 16 yards from the goal-line or back-line. Recently, players have been taking the push or hit nearer to 20 yards from the goal-line or back-line. This should not be permitted.

Efficient umpiring will do much to raise the whole standard of the game at all levels by training players to observe the Rules. An umpire should therefore have a thorough knowledge of the Rules and should be studying them frequently to refresh his memory. He should help in the enjoyment of the games he umpires and should endeavour to interpret the Rules so that each and every game is played in the right spirit.

There are, however, four paramount considerations:

(1) an umpire must obtain and retain complete control of a game.

(2) an umpire must never allow an advantage to be gained by a breach of the Rules.

(3) the whistle should be used as sparingly as possible.

(4) An umpire should co-operate at all times with his colleague to ensure consistency of application, interpretation and effectiveness of the Rules.

It is a mistaken idea that it is the duty of an umpire to penalise every breach of the Rules, as this may cause undue delay and irritation. When no advantage results to the offender, it is unnecessary for an umpire to penalise minor infringements. But once the advantage rule has been put into operation the original breach must be ignored.

As soon as the players realise that they have an umpire who means to enforce the Rules, it will generally be found that rough and dangerous play will cease. Once let a game get out of hand and it will be difficult to pull it together afterwards. In general, players should be given the impression that if they try to co-operate, an umpire will interrupt the flow of the game only when essential for its fair and proper conduct. Kept a calm and impersonal attitude to the game. Concentrate at all times so that nothing outside the game has power to distract your attention.

Anticipate the run or flow of the game. No umpire is more useful than the one whose mind is always alert, and who looks beyond the action of the moment and anticipates the next move. Decisions when made should be given decisively and clearly. In certain circumstances a decision must be delayed long enough to give the "advantage rule" time to operate.

Penalties will have greater significance if umpires restrict their use as much as possible to the more serious breaches of the Rule such as obstruction, offside and dangerous or rough play. An efficient umpire is not, however, one who is over lenient, and play contrary to the spirit of the Rules must be severely dealt with in the interests of the players and the game itself. It is considered that umpires do not make sufficient use of their power to award penalty corners for deliberate breaches within their own 25-yards area, nor o the power to award penalty strokes for deliberate breaches in the circle.

Umpires' Clothing

An umpire should wear clothing:

(a) to allow free movement.

(b) of a colour differing from that of both teams,

(c) with pockets for his equipment, and with

(d) shoes suitable to cope with the field and conditions of the event.

(e) an eyeshade or peaked cap, in preference to dark glasses to cope with strong sunlight.

Dark glasses some time distort-colours and make it difficult to distinguish the different clothing of the two teams.

(f) for protection against bad weather when necessary.

Umpires' Equipment

An umpire should have with him:

(a) a current book of Rules,

(b) a loud distinctive whistle, worn on a cord on a wrist, and a second or reserve whistle.

(c) a stop watch and/or a reliable watch with a second hand,

(d) two pencils,

(e) a card on which to record the starting times of each half the time of suspension of any player and the goals as scored.

Positioning

It is most important for the umpire to be in the correct position to see all breaches of the Rules. To do this he should keep on the move outside the field of play, beyond the side-line with the defending goal on his right, in his own half except when the ball is in the circle or on the far side of the field, when he should move into the field of play and if necessary into the circle itself. From there the umpire can, for example, ensure that for a shot at goal the ball has been hit inside the circle, and will obtain a good view of such offences as obstruction and stick interference. An umpire must be constantly on the move not only to ensure that he is in the correct position according to the state of the game, but also to judge instantly the relative position of the various players at any moment. It is obviously impossible for one who remains stationary always to give the correct decision. It is generally recognised that the most suitable position for the umpire is on the right wing of the attack in his half of the field.

Off-side decisions correct positioning is even more vital. Being level with or slightly nearer the goal than the second defender is strongly recommended. Alternatively be level with or slightly ahead of the attacker with the ball. This is advisable when such an attacker has already passed the second defender. In either case, one advantage will be that any attacking player on the umpire's right is invariably in an off-side position.

Whistling

The whistle should always be blown decisively and loudly enough for all players to hear it. It should not normally be blown for the taking of free hits, 16-yards hits, hit-ins, corners and penalty corners. In rare cases it may be advisable to reverse a decision if it is obvious that a mistake has been made, but this must be done at once or not at all.

Signalling

Take note of the recommended signals given on code of signals for umpires and those occasions when a signal is not always required.

In general the main signal will be the direction one, given with one arm only and that arm raised slightly above the horizontal, with the open palm of the hand at face level.

(1) the award of a goal, when both arms are pointed towards the centre spot;

(2) indicating a breach of the off-side rule, when the first signal is the right arm pointed horizontally across the field;

(3) the award of a 16-yard hit when both arms are extended out side ways;

(4) the award of a penalty corner when both arms are pointed towards the goal.

(5) the award of a penalty stroke, when one arm is pointed upwards and the other pointed to the 7-yard spot;

(6) signalling of a stoppage of time when both arms are crossed above the head.

Signals should be maintained long enough to ensure that all players are aware of the decision.

To become a good umpire requires regular and assiduous practice. The essential qualities of a good umpire, such as mental alertness, decisiveness and a good sense of judgement can be developed and strengthened in this way. If he has made a mistake an umpire should not be discouraged—there is no such thing as a perfect umpire- he must dismiss the mistake from his mind and concentrate still more.

The above advises to umpires is not intended to be comprehensive, but offers general guidance towards a good standard of umpiring.

Field of Play

It is advisable for umpires to make a careful study of the Plan and to check that the ground markings are in accordance with the plan and in particular to check:

(a) the circle markings.

(b) that flag posts are correctly placed and that they are of the correct height.

Posts under 4 ft. in height are dangerous. It should be noted that all boundary lines are within the field of play.

Hockey Terminology

Playing the Ball: Playing the ball is stopping or moving the ball with the stick in any manner or, in the case of the goalkeeper, with the foot, hand or any part of the body.

A Stroke: A "Stroke" is executed when the ball has been moved by playing striking or deflecting it.

A Hit: A "hit" is a stroke with a swinging movement of the stick in order to increase the ball's speed.

A Push: A "Push" moves the ball along the ground by a pushing movement of the stick after the stick has been placed close to a stationary or rolling ball. When a push is made, both the ball and head of the stick are in contact with the ground.

The Flick: A Flick occurs when a stationary or rolling ball is pushed and, as a result, is raised off the ground.

The Scoop: A "scoop" occurs when a stationary or nearly motionless ball is raised off the ground by means of a shovel-movement of the stick, after the head o the stick is placed slightly under the ball.

A Shot at Goal: Any stroke by an attacker within the circle towards goal.

Pass-back: The pass-back is a push or hit not directed over the centre-line, which means the ball must be player either square or in any backward direction.

Playing Distance: Playing distance is the distance within which a player is capable of playing the ball. The playing distance will depend upon the reach of the player involved.

If the Rules require players to remain beyond playing distance of the ball, the players are not allowed to play, approach, or attempt to play the ball until it has been played or touched by another player of either team.

INDEX